From a Soldier's Diary

From a Soldier's Diary

S.A. D'Amore, Colonel USAF
(Retired)

VANTAGE PRESS
New York

FIRST EDITION

Published by Vantage Press, Inc.
419 Park Ave. South, New York, NY 10016

Manufactured in the United States of America
ISBN: 978-0-533-16226-0

Library of Congress Catalog Card No: 2009903215

0 9 8 7 6 5 4 3 2 1

In memory of Mildred Rose O'Donnell D'Amore,
my wife for 62 years

From a Soldier's Diary

I

My life began on the twenty-third of October in the year of 1916. With good fortune and health, in spite of some changes, it still goes on in this year of 2009.

Early in my life my hair was the color of anthracite coal . . . black. Now it is the color of newly fallen snow . . . white. In my prime, I stood tall at five feet and eleven inches. Now, if I stretch forcibly, I reach five feet ten inches . . . um, closer to nine. Anyway, before Mother Nature wrings an additional toll, and I undergo other changes during my continuing life and living process, I wish to tell this story, which is more a review of selective memories related to occasions and events met during the execution of my commission in military service. Knowingly, a shadowy veil is waved over the illstarred and trying situations.

I entered high school in 1929 when the future looked rosy. I graduated when the Great Depression laid siege to my small town Freeland, Pennsylvania . . . It was time for me to face the real world and fight the foreboding odds.

My first job was with the government-sponsored Works Project Administration (WPA). The name had a lofty ring. In a sense, it did turn out to be lofty... I was required to loft a ten-pound sledgehammer and strike large rocks until they were crumbled into small stones for use in the construction of public roads. I swung that hammer for six agonizing months.

Because of my dedication and my high school diploma, I was transferred to a job with the Bureau of Entomology and Plant Quarantine, Department of Agriculture. To me, that sounded like a chance to move up the ladder. It was, as it turned out, I was required to affix climbing spikes to the calves of my legs and shinny to the top of huge, tall trees to eradicate our prey . . . the gypsy moth. I climbed countless trees for twelve long months.

Although these government-sponsored jobs paid me only thirty dollars a month, they did spare me the humiliation of being placed on the Relief Rolls. However I knew I had to enter a more productive field. I wasn't the only one that was forced into such a boundless state. Others, like myself, sensed that if we stayed put, we would be strangled to a point where we would be stymied and unable to move beyond the prevailing social, political and intellectual character of the beleaguered town. Consequently, like the burst of a huge circular spray of fireworks, we finally darted in all directions to take on a more promising life.

I opted for the resort area of Miami Beach, Florida. Within two years, I became recognized as a successful restaurateur and personage of a supper club.

After spending a rewarding and instructive two years in the resort area of Miami Beach, I visualized a span of fame on the horizon as a highly successful restaurateur. I decided to visit the west coast and cap that dream in the glamorous area of Los Angeles, California. Sadly, after my arrival, it all turned out to be an illusion. All I saw on the horizon were the ever-increasing clouds of war. Slowly, reality and patriotism began to take hold, so I returned to the east coast, and on 15 April 1941, volunteered to enlist, as a private, in the Regular Army of the United States.

My friends found it hard to accept the fact that I would join the regular army, the reason being that from the spring of 1932, tolerance for a man in the military uniform had taken a nose dive. That was when approximately 22,000 World War I veterans, calling themselves the Bonus Expeditionary Force, banded together and marched into the city of Washington, D.C. to demand an early payment of the $1,424 bonus they had been promised in return for their service during the Great War. Congress refused the immediate payment, and stuck to its original payment date of 1952. The bonus army stood fast, and set up encampments in and around the city. With time, the state of camps became appalling. The unpleasant conditions disturbed the high officials in the administration. An order was given to a group of active professional soldiers to dispel the veterans. Following orders, 843 infantrymen, led by Major Dwight D. Eisenhower and Major George S. Patton, rammed into the veterans, shouting obscenities while striking and trampling them. Inevitably they pushed the veterans out of the city. A great segment of the U.S. citizenry placed the blame for the craven behavior on *all* active duty soldiers, including General Douglas MacArthur, the officer who gave the order. As a result, respect for the uniform was lost, and those wearing it were shunned and scorned. The people turned their attention to the popular radio programs that starred Amos and Andy, The Shadow, Jack Benny, and to the music of Guy Lombardo, Cab Calloway and Paul Whiteman, while shrugging off all military matters including the bombing of London and the occupation of Paris by the Nazis.

Nevertheless, standing with five other enlistees, I stood as straight as the flagstaff in the corner of the room and took the oath to serve. The switch from civilian to military status was accomplished in a hasty, five-minute ceremony. Immediately after the lackluster ritual, the six of us were assigned to the Army Air Corps, which was a new branch of the twenty-two branches of the newly designed United States Army. At the same time, I was given a packet of papers, six train tickets, a book of vouchers and instructed to get on the train, lead the others and report for duty at McDill Field, Tampa, Florida.

The morning after our arrival at McDill Field, my role as a leader came to an abrupt end. Along with my temporary charges, the six of us were assembled with several other enlistees and summarily assigned to the "Rake Brigade."

An old-time, gruff sergeant appeared and addressed us with a grumpy and guttural voice, saying, "Okay, you recruits, let's start this beautiful day of ours with a little, simple exercise. I want you rookies to grab a rake from yonder shed and start cleaning this compound and rid it of all the debris. Got It? Then, LET'S GO!"

One by one, the enlistees dutifully peeled off from the group to claim a rake and began to comb the clean sandy ground and rid it of the phantasmal debris. I stood fast. When the sergeant saw that I didn't move, he shouted, "Hey rookie, are you deaf or dumb? I didn't excuse you! I ordered *all* of you to grab a tool and rake this compound. Now get your ass going."

Pleadingly and defensively I said, "Sergeant, I'm still wearing my best civilian suit that I wore when I reported here yesterday. I don't want to soil it. I will gladly do anything you order as soon as I am issued a uniform."

"Well," he growled with his face almost touching mine, "Now along with you mamma boys we are blessed with a prima donna in this here new army." Then he blasted with, "Cut the crap and get your dainty ass behind a rake RIGHT NOW!"

I didn't move and quietly said, "Not until I get to wear an army uniform."

"Hey, wise ass, what you're gonna get is company punishment for disobeying my direct order. You will soon learn not to frig round with me or any other noncom." He grabbed and held onto my arm as he shoved me ahead toward the orderly room. Once inside the office, he described the confrontation, word for word, to the major who was in command of the unit. When he completed the recitation, the major, seemingly perplexed, said, "Sergeant, you did right to bring this to my attention. I will take disciplinary action that will straighten him out. You may go back to your post and leave him to me."

When the sergeant left the room, the major turned to face me, sighed and in an appeasing manner said, "Young man, first off, I want you to know that these old-time, line-sergeants are superb in their trade. At times, some tend to perform their duties in an egocentric manner, especially now that they have a bunch of new recruits to impress with their leadership position." He stopped speaking and appeared to fall into deep thought. Several seconds later, while wearing the faint beginnings of a pleased smile, said with slow-paced words, "I must show the sergeant my support for discipline, so I'm going to include you with the small group of airplane mechanics that is being transferred to a new airfield up north. Anyway, I'm sure the transfer will greatly benefit you."

Dale Mabry Field, Tallahassee, Florida was not complete in form, equipment or personnel. When I arrived it held a cadre of several hundred noncommissioned officers that was busy putting the field in order. Instantly, I was welcomed to pitch in as a needed helping hand. As the work progressed, the noncoms became satisfied with my work and took me under their wings and taught and trained me to become one of their own. . . . A Regular Army Man.

The year of 1941 had already arrived with a bang. Then it burst forth like a volcanic eruption. . . . President Roosevelt was inaugurated for a third time; the Lend Lease for Arms bill was passed; the USO was formed to cater to the Armed Forces; Jimmy Stewart, the Hollywood idol was inducted into the service; Stalin was named Premier of Soviet Russia; and thus the days continued to race past at full gallop.

On 6 April 1941, the New York Herald Tribune carried the headline GERMANS MARCH ON YUGOSLAVIA AND GREECE. Yugoslavia surrendered. On 27 April the swastika flew from the Acropolis in Athens. All of this happened in spite of the assurance from the European generals that Yugoslavia was impregnable because a precipitous mountain terrain made it unsuitable for a German blitzkrieg operation. Also they assured the world that Greece was protected because there were three British divisions stationed there. But Hitler overcame all of it! Now the line sergeants dubbed the European generals "old and bewildered fogies." The more seasoned old-timers were not as kind. They called them plain "stupid."

On 20 June 1941, the Army Air Force (AAF) was established. The Air Corps became a subordinate element of the AAF. The old-timers were beginning to shake off the title soldier for that of airman. Two days later the world was shocked to hear that Germany had attacked her strong ally, Russia. Winston Churchill was pleased by the move and declared Britain's full support for Russia.

Progress toward the attainment of a full, authorized complement at Dale Mabry was going along at full speed. However, weaponry training lagged behind. The reason for that set-back could reasonably be attributed to the fact that immediately after the signing of the Armistice on 11 November 1918, Congress pulled the plug on the Army's arms, equipment and manpower, thereby reducing its stature to a point where the United States Army ranked sixteenth in the world . . . right behind Romania. Be that as it may, we newcomers, prompted and prodded by the hovering and demanding noncommissioned officers, endured a part of that dilemma. When we were not employed on a work detail, or peeling potatoes, or attending lectures, or viewing instructive military films, we assembled and disassembled and fired the M-1 rifle and the 45-caliber pistol until we became proficient with both.

As the explosive and unrestrained year went on, the continuing build-up of personnel forced quite a few promotions. In the midst the whirlpool of actions, and aided with the constant care and training given by the noncoms, I was promoted from private to private first class; corporal; sergeant; staff sergeant; technical sergeant; and acting first sergeant.

The day on which I received the rank of staff sergeant I entered that eminent and enduring troop of soldiers officially referred as the First-Three-Graders. This key group included staff sergeants, technical sergeants, first sergeants, and master sergeants. Commissioned officers and enlisted men accepted each as a seasoned soldier and a capable leader. Honoring the rank, a first-three-grader was excused from the run-of-the-mill assignments and was allowed the special privilege to get married without military permission. Brusque line sergeants steered away from marriage, gruffly maintaining that a wife was either a luxury, or worse, a hindrance. They cited one of their old sayings, "If the army wanted you to have a wife, it would have issued you one."

One of my honored duties as a first-three-grader was that in the absence of the first sergeant, I was permitted to sit with and help the commander at the pay table on payday. Payday fell on the last day of each month. It was recognized as a soldier's holiday. Generally the commander of the unit, the fist sergeant, and the orderly sat behind a long table. The troops formed a line in alphabetical order. At the appointed time, each man approached the table to state his name. The orderly would reconcile the name with his roster. If all were in order, he would call out "Check." That word signaled to the soldier to move along to the commander, who would dole out the pay, after deducting the money due from the soldier for his indebtedness for laundry, dry cleaning, theatre coupons—and the perennial donations of twenty-five cents for the Old Soldier's Home. At that point the line ended for most soldiers. For some, old and new alike, there was an additional person to face, the unit shylock. Every unit had its moneylender who would gladly loan money to a GI for whatever reason. Of course the interest rate was high, generally 45 percent of the amount borrowed. After satisfying all of his honorable obligations, the GI would clutch the remainder of his meager monthly stipend and wave it in the air and joyfully broadcast, "The Eagle shit! The Eagle shit!" Then he would rush off to some glorious land to satisfy his pent-up amoral desires. To show the world that they were men, most of them would make their way to the Post Exchange to buy and smoke cigarettes. The younger they were, the sooner they began the habit. Those who needed encouragement were influenced by the multitude of endorsements made by famous personalities such as Joe DiMaggio, baseball's hero of the day. The army seduced the others by offering cigarettes at an exceptionally low cost. The PX prominently displayed cartons upon cartons of Camels, Lucky Strikes, Chesterfields, and Old Gold's for sixty-five cents a carton or seven cents a pack.

The Selective Training and Service Act, which was made law in 1940, now was in full swing and geared for an annual conscription of 900,000 men to serve in the Army for one year. It had already started to pump hundreds of men to all existing military installations, causing family disruptions nation-wide. Still, the general public gave little attention to consequential and portentous outgrowth of the military undertakings, and gave less attention to the significant changes that were being wrought around the globe. Surprisingly, they failed to recognize the threatening and imminent war clouds that were on the horizon and rapidly moving westward.

Fourteen months after I enlisted in the Regular Army, I submitted an application for entrance in an officer candidate school, which was scheduled to open and groom selected personnel for a commission as a Second Lieutenant in the Army.

In 1942, the application was honored and with fifty-nine other aspirants, entered the school as a candidate to compete for a commission as a Second Lieutenant. After being enrolled, all candidates had to undergo additional testing, schooling and training for ninety days to determine if, we were worthy to receive that important and honored commission.

On the nineteenth day, October 17, 1942, the great moment arrived when I raised my right hand and repeated a soldier's oath:

"I, Stanley A. D'Amore, having been appointed a Second Lieutenant in the Army of the United States, do solemnly swear that I will support and defend the Constitution of the United States against all enemies, foreign and domestic; that I will bear true faith and allegiance to the same; that I take this obligation freely, without any mental reservation or purpose of evasion; and that I will and faithfully discharge the duties of the office upon which I am about to enter, SO HELP ME GOD."

At that moment, the Officer Candidate School (OCS) Classification, 101, was shed for the commissioned officer classification, Second Lieutenant: 01. At that point, I joined the ranks of officers who were charged with the dual duty to lead men and to restore peace under conditions acceptable to the people of the nation. My initial duty assignment was with the Air Corps at a new airfield carved out of a huge remote tract of sandy and marshy palmetto-covered prairie located about seven miles southwest of Sebring, Florida. Because of the frenzy and need given to the operational readiness of the flight line, there was no time for traditional military ceremonies. Consequently, I was dutifully and politely brushed aside and unceremoniously directed to take command of a detachment of sixty recruits, as directed by the War Department order that sent me to Hendricks Field, and join the small nucleus of the highly trained personnel that had been selected to establish a school to train and coordinate combat crews for the B-17 Flying Fortress. I, like all newcomers, was compelled to dig in and work by fixed course of past patterns to accommodate the specific facets called for in the stated mission. Not one of us complained, asked why or wavered. Soldier pride and know-how drove us on.

Stanley A. D'Amore, 2nd Lieutenant. The day I was commissioned.

Prior to my arrival, the detachment of sixty men had been attached to an aviation squadron and administered to by Captain Josiah Macon, a member of the Personnel Division. Macon was a reserve officer who, until six months previously, was employed as a clerk in a rural court house north of Savannah, Georgia. He was fifty-something years old and had a body that would be classified as a bit more than chubby. His shirt collar, about size 15, was drawn tight around his neck, about size 16, causing a red neck and a flushed round face to pop out like a bubble ready to burst. He sat behind a scarred, green-colored metal desk heaped with army manuals and bulletins. A hand-carved wooden sign sat front and center on his desk giving notice to his position, Administrator of Records. It was a duty that would turn out to be long lasting for him in that shortly after his arrival on duty he incurred and injury that required constant monitoring by the local medical staff. His seemingly secure position helped to stoke a blustering and self-important carriage. He demonstrated these weaknesses when he made an awkward and feeble attempt to welcome me.

"Son . . . they call you Stan, don't they? You should feel honored that you were given command of a Truck Transportation Detachment on your first duty assignment. Command is the most challenging duty, even for us old-timers, and those who graduate from *long-term* military school." He stopped talking for a moment, shaking his head, silently questioning the action that gave a brand-new second lieutenant a position of command. Then, taking a deep breath and expelling it loudly through pursed lips, he warned, "In your case, it's going to be most difficult. *All sixty* of your men are new, raw recruits. Only ten of them are above average. You might use those fellows to help organize your outfit. But don't expect too much. The class of people you will be dealing with lack the ability to comprehend the technical aspects of the mission we are dealing with here." He let that opinion hang in the air as fact. To dull the sting of his tactless statement, he patronizingly added, "Yet, all sixty *look* like good boys and I am sure some of them have the makings of good soldiers . . . even though they are black."

It was easy to read the bias in the captain's spiel. It assured me that it wasn't the tight shirt collar that gave him a red neck. The captain clearly had shown that he was a gullible supporter of faiths of a provincial community where it was perceived that a Negro was less able to perform in any capacity other than tilling the soil, and not qualified to overcome technical or academic problems.

Getting no opening from me to continue with his unfavorable image of Negro soldiers, the captain shifted to a new jackstraw. He picked up my record and poked with a questioning voice, "I see your personnel file . . . your 201 . . . says you shot up through the enlisted ranks from Buck Private to Acting First Sergeant in a little more than one year. You must have been one hell of a soldier!" He shot a brief look of disbelief in my direction and continued, "Then you got a commission at an Officer Candidate School in just ninety days . . . *and then given an assignment of command?*" He contorted his face and summed up the review with a jeering and sneering one word, "Wow!"

I sloughed off the intended derision with a flippant comment, "Yeah, I was pretty damn lucky, I guess."

The captain didn't yield with his intended put down; he dug further. "Well, I'll admit that some old sergeants do well in handling certain minor duties of an officer, but as a commanding office on an initial duty assignment. . . . " The rising pitch of his conjectural words hung there for an instant. I felt it was time to squelch further mocking, and interrupted.

"Oh, I think I know what you mean," I said, "Hell, I've met captains who could *never* pull the duties of a buck-ass sergeant. But, that's the Army fur yuh!" I sighed and shook my head in mocked wonderment. That ended the conversation.

My number one task was to transform a ten-acre plot of vacant land into a sturdy compound to pool the fleet of vehicles that was assigned to the Detachment, including fifty heavy duty trucks, twenty jeeps and twelve supercharged motorcycles. First, the spongy ground had to be stabilized to support the weight of the trucks. Then, it was necessary to build an office to house the vehicle dispatcher and the truckmaster. Disturbingly, the Detachment did not have the resources nor the priority to get immediate assistance from the Post Engineer. Providentially, a salvage yard sat contiguous to the ten-acre plot of land. In it were miscellaneous pieces of surplus lumber that were stored for future use, and huge slabs of concrete that had been rejected and removed from the airstrip because they did not meet the dynamic impaction tests for aircraft runways.

Conjuring a crafty scheme, I hopped on a new motorcycle and zoomed down the road to the chief engineer's office and stopped it near the entrance of his building. Faking a problem, I revved up the engine to the maximum and held it there for five seconds before letting it drop back to idle. The action was repeated about five times, making it appear it was being done to check a faulty rhythm of the engine. The rise and fall of the roaring engine finally called for attention. The head of the engineering department, a major, stepped out onto a small veranda of his office. Visibly annoyed, he stood there in silence watching while the throttle was being manipulated. About to complain about the roaring racket, he shouted, "You got a problem, Lieutenant?"

"Not really," I mumbled with a pained tone of voice and head cocked toward the roaring engine, "I just received twelve of these beauties and I'm checking this one and fine-tuning it." Then with faked concern, murmured, "Sounds like this one needs an adjustment before I assign it to someone."

"Are you telling me that you, a brand new second lieutenant, control their assignment?" The question was loaded with doubt.

"Yeah . . . part of my job," I sighed as if agonized with the responsibility.

"How do you determine who is authorized to have one?" Now this question was infused with hope.

"Well, there are some broad guidelines to follow. In spite of that, I just got rid of the tenth one on the flight line. Got two left and want to assign them by the end of the week."

"Boy," the major expressed his wish, "I sure as hell would love to have one of those babies. Make my job a lot easier running all-around checking all the engineering projects."

That did it. With an informal agreement of reciprocity, a motorcycle was assigned to the chief engineer for his official use. In return, he was to make delivery of the slabs of concrete and truckloads of lumber to the swampy site, then help the detachment personnel to lay the slabs of concrete to form a solid compound on which to accommodate approximately one hundred heavy duty vehicles. In addition, he agreed to oversee the erection of an office building for the use of the truck dispatcher, truckmaster and their crews.

The extensive projects were completed by mid-November. Staggered by the enthusiasm and performance of the sixty raw recruits, I sponsored a party for them and their family members. The sixty men, and a collective total of twenty-five relatives, indulged in the informal, shirtsleeve gathering.

On 1 November 1942, a command-wide briefing was held pertaining to the current war events in the European Theatre of Operations. The uplifting news during the hour-long session pertained to General Bernard Montgomery, Commander of the British 8th Army, fighting in the desert of North Africa. It was learned that on 23 October 1942, Montgomery had made an earthshaking advancement by blasting his way through the elaborate and heavily seeded German mine field, known as Devil Garden, located on the edge of El Alamein. The commander of the German forces, General Erwin Rommel, fought ferociously to stand firm against Montgomery's British forces. He couldn't. He was beaten and retreated. In the end, he lost a sizeable segment of his infantry and motorized units. *This battle turned out to be a paramount victory for the Allies.*

Despite a promotion to First Lieutenant, Officer Classification: 02, the accomplishments, the excitement and honor of command, I felt incomplete. Twenty months from the time of my enlistment in the Regular Army, I proposed marriage to Mildred O'Donnell, a hometown sweetheart, and was married on the day after Christmas, 1942.

Millie, as she was affectionately known, had a delicately molded face that heralded her beauty. But it was her spirit and character that made her loved by everyone. She was born into an Irish family that was steeped with strong Irish influence. It was not easy for a "Non-Irish" pursuer to invade such a family and carry away one of its maidens—but this Italian did.

After a short leave of absence, a current events briefing revealed that Joseph Stalin, the Dictator of the USSR and Commander-in-Chief of its Armed Forces, had advocated the promulgation of war plans that were not in harmony with those touted by President Roosevelt and British's Prime Minister, Winston Churchill. The radical deflection in the strategy of the two plans caused tension and stalled the Churchill-Roosevelt plan that called for an attack on the European continent. Despite the impasse, American commanders were advised to accelerate training programs and prepare their forces for the impending invasion of Europe. The prodding was well directed and gainful. Combat readiness was heightened. That in place, Roosevelt and Churchill, with their top military leaders, met in Casablanca to finalize the agreement to cross the English Channel and attack the German axis. *Later* Stalin agreed.

During that critical time, many officers and men arrived at Hendricks Field and just as many left, most for exciting overseas assignments. The great majority of the officers that departed had spent far less time on Hendricks than my seventeen months. I felt sidetracked and pressed the Personnel Division for a reason. Captain Macon, as an administrator, was involved in the records review. His opening welcome was a smart-mouth comment, "Well, here is the white knight of sixty black boys and one hundred shiny trucks. Hey, it sure looks like you are destined to be a fixture right here for the duration!

Some of the fellows already refer to you as Mister Hendricks the Homesteader."

Ignoring the captain, an ardent appeal was directed to the Chief of Personnel begging him to contact higher headquarters and learn the cause for the long delay. The Chief empathized with me. He agreed that the prolongation of my tour on Hendricks Field was unusual. To help, he made an official query in the name of the commanding general. An initial review of the records simply revealed the ordinary and routine facts pertaining to a transfer of station. However, a further review indicated that an oversight was committed.

"Stan," the Chief of Personnel said, "Good thing we dug into this. Having been assigned for duty with an all-black detachment, a SNAFU down the line mistakenly carried you as a Negro officer. As you know, because of the segregation policy, Negro officers are moved about only through War Department orders. If that error had not been found and corrected, you probably have had to stay with the Detachment. Regardless, the mystery has been solved and you should hear the results very soon."

As predicted, a short time later I was assigned to Project Zebbra-0228, and transferred to Kelly Field, San Antonio, Texas. The nature of the assignment prohibited accompaniment of dependents. Millie returned to Freeland, Pennsylvania "for the duration."

The war in Europe was swinging in favor of the allies, especially in Italy. The Italians already had shunned Mussolini's goals and cast him aside in disgrace and discredit. However, the war continued to rage within Italy. On 1 October, the U.S. 5th Army, commanded by General Mark Clark, entered Naples, and the British 8th Army, commanded by General Bernard Montgomery, entered

Millie on the day she departed Hendricks Field for Freeland, Pennsylvania.

Foggia. In the meantime, the Allies bombed and completely destroyed the Monte Cassino Abbey, transforming it into heaps of rubble, stone and concrete. These devastating events began to shatter the spirit if the Italian soldiers. They lost battles before; now they manifested a loss of interest in the war, shouting, "*Che peccato . . . Basta! Basta!*" The Allies recognized the vulnerability of the tottering forces and "invited" them to exact satisfaction for the wrong that was perpetrated by Mussolini and his association with Germany. It worked. On 13 October 1943, Italy declared war on Germany. The Italian troops joined the Allies as co-belligerents.

I entered Project Zebbra-0228 at Kelly Field on 9 March 1944, and was given command of the newly constituted and newly activated, 2249th Transportation Truck Company (Aviation). Its table of organization and equipment (T/O AND E) called for a commander, two officers, ninety-nine enlisted men, a long list of cargo trucks, and a great amount of maintenance equipment. The two assigned officers, First Lieutenant Cliff Newlin and First Lieutenant Robert Gillespie, were qualified for duty with a truck company. However, the assigned enlisted men were not trained to perform the required tasks nor were they familiar with, or qualified to use, the equipment and vehicles. Worse yet, they were lacking passion, perhaps for a rational reason, in that they were part of the innocent, disappointed, and confused bunch of men that had been shunted from one installation to another and finally collected at Kelly Field where they faultlessly formed a pool of replacements for any understaffed unit, regardless of their required training or qualification.

Saddling a unit with a few soldiers to perform tasks foreign to their basic skills was no big deal. They would meld into the unit without a problem. In this case, however, *ninety percent* of those assigned to the company were not schooled or qualified to perform the required tasks. Despite this appalling handicap and the incomplete complement of authorized vehicles and equipment, orders directed that action be taken to shape the men into a proper functional unit without delay because *it was scheduled to move to the New York port of embarkation within thirty-seven days to join the mobilization forces for the impending invasion of Europe.*

To ease the imbalance of personnel, I begged for a handful of qualified people, but was not successful. In fact, it was made known that because of the urgent push, many commanders would face the same problem. Caution and foresight steered me to make the situation a matter of record and send a letter to the Commanding General. In part, the letter stated:

> I wish to say I am honored to be in command of a unit that is earmarked for an important mission. However, I respectfully request action be taken to alleviate the abysmal composition of my company, in that it carries over eighty percent of personnel that are malassigned for the mission.
>
> S.A. D'Amore, First Lieutenant
> Commanding Officer
> 2249 Quartermaster Truck Company (Aviation)

A couple of days later a reply was received.

Subject: Status of Personnel 1 April 1944
To: Commanding Officer
Quartermaster Truck Co. (Avn)
Kelly Field, Texas

1. In the organization of your unit, it is realized that enlisted men have been assigned thereto with MOS (Military Occupational Specialty) numbers that are not authorized for your unit.

2. For your information, these assignments were made upon the approval of such procedures by the Commanding General, Air Service Command, Patterson Field, Ohio, who had coordinated this with the Commanding General, Army Air Force, Washington, D.C.

By Command of Brigadier General Vanaman
Gervis J. Garner, Colonel, Air Corps
Chief, Personnel and Training Division

Because the majority of the men had not undergone rigid basic training, having been shunted from post to post seemingly unwanted, they had become apathetic, lethargic and indolent. With only days before embarkation, it was unquestionably necessary to energize them and develop them into straight-arrow soldiers to react instantly to the will of their leaders. A rigorous training program was designed to achieve the goals. Progress was slow and discouraging. The men were savvy and certainly had the basic inborn means, but they were not responding positively. Weighing this dilemma, I concluded there was good reason for me to act outside the existing bounds of the military rules and regulations that were imposed by the army. I decided to use deviant tactics and sidestep those stifling rules, just as I had done as a sergeant, when *shock treatment was the quickest solution to the attitude problem.*

On the sixteenth of April, the day before shipping to the port of embarkation, I gave a brusque order to the first sergeant.

"Arrange a clothing and equipment 'shakedown' inspection for tonight at twenty-one hundred hours. Have the men display *all* gear and clothing in their possession." Then, turning to the two lieutenants, "You two will accompany me. Bring along a can of gasoline and a cardboard box." A rapid departure left no room for questions or comments.

At nine o'clock that night, the shakedown inspection was conducted inside the barracks. Seventy-nine men met the required clothing and equipment standards. From the other twenty, all unauthorized items and gear, such as service caps, army jump boots, britches and helmets were appropriated and neatly placed in the cardboard box. One half hour later, the inspection was complete and the men were assembled in the compound outside the barracks.

"Men, ten days ago I *informed* you that we were about to embark for Europe on a serious mission. I *told* you we were *directed* to travel with *only* government-issued clothing, gear, and equipment. Because of that, I *ordered* you to swap, sell, send home, or get rid of all non-issued items immediately." After a short pause, and with a distressed tone, I continued, "Instead, some of you hung onto your old sluggish ways, ignoring that prerequisite and my orders. I know you feel like black sheep as a result of being shunted from post to post and finally landing into a new unit to do a job for which you were not trained. I understood your feelings and, therefore, I tolerated your lollygagging." Another pause, then loudly, "But no more! There will be no more assdragging! Those who disobey orders, who lag behind, who act indifferently will suffer a penalty commensurate with the violation."

Having said that, the contents of the cardboard box was dumped onto the ground, and splashed with gasoline. I tossed a lighted match into the heap. The men moaned and muttered, chocking out guttural words, as the flames devoured the pile of unauthorized items. "Let this be a *tiny* example of the penalty you will pay whenever you disobey official orders!" *That was the first deviant action taken.*

On the return to the orderly room, Lieutenant Gillespie said, "Sir, don't you fear any flack from higher up? What you just did is definitely against army regulations."

"Bob, the shakedown was purposely scheduled this late at night. It's after ten o'clock. Most of the brass have already knocked off and are in the sack for the night. Tomorrow we'll be in Camp Shanks, New York, headed for England before anyone gets wind of it. Anyway, it's a small price to pay to make the men know that I mean business."

The following morning the company was berthed on a troop ship and swallowed into a hold that was already jam-packed with a mass of army troops. Hammocks hung side by side, head to toe, in triple tiers, from one bulkhead to the other, giving the appearance of a sea of huge trampolines. After some grousing, inane jokes began bouncing back and forth among the occupants.

"One good thing about being so crowded, it doesn't leave enough room for a fart to fly and stink up the joint."

"Yeah . . . but just pray that the guy in the upper sack doesn't get sick and puke down all over ya!"

"We're so far below deck, I feel like I'm in a submarine. When the hell do we go up for air?"

"When we dock, dummy, in about two hundred forty hours. Then, if we're lucky, we will get to go upstairs for some air."

"Upstairs? Hey, jerk, ya better talk the navy lingo or we'll be stuffed down here forever."

So it went until the ship got underway. It was then

when everyone awakened and realized that they were embarking on a risky and dangerous journey. They switched words and thoughts to bothersome uncertainties. My troublesome concern was centered on the readiness of the men committed to my care. Time was vital. The men could not be allowed to loll about and goldbrick during the estimated ten-day journey. Sharing that persistent problem with the ship's officers, a request was made for permission to assemble the men on open deck where they could continue with their schooling. The request was granted. The men were grateful. Their one-day ordeal in the crowded hold, suffocated by the rank body and food odors, was enough to make them eager to get up on the open deck, even if it was to *train* and *study*.

For days the troop ship zigzagged across the Atlantic, obviously to avoid enemy action. Throughout that time, firm and purposeful training continued under the competent coaching of Lieutenants Newlin and Gillespie.

Lieutenant Robert Gillespie, the Company Adjutant was a native of Pocatello, Idaho. He graduated from Idaho State University, reported to active duty as an officer and assigned to the truck company. He was an easygoing person, flexible with all commonplace things, but not as the Company Adjutant. He was a firm leader and a strict adherent to army regulation. One of his additional duties—*all officers had additional duties*—was Company Censor. The task of the censor was to review outgoing correspondence and delete anything that might compromise military security.

The day before the ship reached Liverpool, England, Gillespie requested a private meeting.

"Sir, I wanted to see you alone before going ashore.

As the company censor, I have a very disturbing matter that bothers me."

"Shoot, Bob. This is a good time to do it. Starting early in the morning, we'll be busy as hell and won't have time for easy chitchat."

"Sir, I've spent most of my spare time on the crossing censoring close to a thousand letters. I have them ready to drop in the mail just as soon as we get into port."

"I know. I saw the sacks."

"But . . . I've been drawn into a knotty situation. The bulk of the letters are routine. They include minor gripes and, for the most part, express love and loneliness. However, one writer has penned some nasty things about you. In a couple of his letters he went so far to state that if he had a chance, you would be his first target."

"Bob, stop right there. I know that as a censor you struggle with how much you should delete and what you should reveal. Say no more. Bob, at this point I am not about to fear what some knucklehead or his buddies say or think about me. Let the letters go forward as written."

The ship dropped anchor at Liverpool. The next morning hundreds of troops began to disembark. There was no joking, no laughing. All wore a pensive look as they carried their heavy duffel bags, slung over their shoulders, and shuffled with uncertain steps down the steep gangplank. On the pier, a sense of urgency permeated the air. Those in charge of administering to the troops were intent on fighting the clock. As each unit was collected and its records processed, it was pushed off the pier and sent on its way to make room for others. Within a couple hours, the 2249th Transportation Company was moved, seemingly with indifference, to a military installation near London where it became a part of the IX Troop Carrier Service Wing.

The installation served as a camp and a processing area. It was far-spreading and held a sea of squad tents. Hundreds of men sat silently in small huddles, holding onto their belongings while listening to the never-ending instructions being preached by their noncommissioned officers. At the same time, the commissioned officers were engaged in a determined businesslike tempo, moving about to make final arrangements for the anticipated order to move out and become part of the tremendous concentration of one hundred thousand troops along the eastern and southern shores of England. The total picture almost disguised every man's immediate torment with the "heebie-jeebies."

The 2249th was not yet indoctrinated in local rules and regulations, therefore higher authority, automatically and properly, restricted its movement for seven days, prohibiting the men to move beyond the perimeter of the installation. During that week, every effort was made to obtain the balance of authorized trucks and equipment that were necessary to reach the state of operational readiness for integration into the selected invading forces. Very little headway was made. Most of the needed items already had been issued to the earlier arrivals. The leftovers were not enough, or of the type, to satisfy our needs. At that point, the 2249th was, in fact, *an impotent company.*

In spite of the weak posture, the training program went on. No man was excused. To ensure their presence, I tacked on an additional seven-day restriction to the *official* one that just ended. Of course, such action violated current army regulations, but once again, I felt compelled to act outside the bounds of rules in order to remedy the unheeding circumstances in which the army had placed me. *That was the second deviant action taken.*

Three weeks from the time we departed New York, on 6 May, I was promoted to Captain, Officer Classification: 03. A week later, on 6 June 1944, less than one month after the company arrived in England, a steady roar of aircraft engines and a seemingly never-ending cloud of aircraft pulled everyone's attention skyward. Formation after formation of approximately 1,000 bombers and troop carriers followed the lead uninterrupted. The 82nd and the 101st Airborne Divisions were on their way to France. *The invasion was on!*

While we were mired in an ineffectual pool, slowly collecting authorized vehicles and equipment, more and more men, equipment and planes headed for the European continent. On 16 June 1944, Lieutenant Newlin certified that *finally* the company was brought to full strength with vehicles and equipment. Ironically, on that day, it was made known that the group with which we would have moved forward, if all trucks and equipment had been on hand, was decimated by German forces.

First Lieutenant Cliff Newlin, the executive officer, carried himself like a storybook army officer and southern gentleman. His commission was immediate and he was directed to the Corps of Engineers. However, exigencies of the service transferred him in short order to the Quartermaster Corps, and finally to the new transportation company. He preformed his duties in a quite, unruffled fashion, never raising his voice in anger or direction. He was a rousing teacher and a successful motivator. When he spoke, the men listened and learned.

Under Newlin's direction, the men became more receptive as they continued to learn more about the 2 ½ ton cargo truck, which was the backbone of the company. The truck carried six driving wheels, two in the front and four in the back. The rear wheels held dual tires. Officially, it was called: "Two and a Half Ton, Six by Six with Four Dual Tires (2 ½ ton, 6x6, 4dt)." The GIs called it a "six by" or a "deuce and a half."

In time, the men learned how to properly maneuver the rugged and powerful "six by" over deep ditches, gullies, and rough terrain; how to negotiate it when under a heavy and oversized load; how to load and lash all types of cargo; how to secure the vehicles onto landing ships; how to read map grids and interpret military and geodetic maps to visualize the configuration and physical features of the terrain; how to perform first and second echelon of maintenance; and how to handle a .50 caliber machine gun when mounted on a moving truck. Everyone was proud of the incredible advancement. Although the men were still learning, they were no longer misfits, *except one.* Early on, this man chose not to participate in the program wholeheartedly. He hung onto the listless behavior he had carried with him to Kelly Field. He continued to complain and belittle issued orders and was slow to perform tasks, with lame excuses for each committed shortcoming. But, he was careful to spout off only when he had a receptive dupe.

"It's against army regs to confine us like this."

"What the hell is he bucking for? Another promotion? Train, train, train. What a crock!"

"If we gotta go through more of this training shit, I'm gonna ask for a transfer to Patton's army and get out of this chickenshit outfit."

"If he didn't have those bars, I wooda kicked his ass all over the friggin lot when he burned my stuff back at Kelly."

"Back on my turf, he would be dead meat."

The field phone gave out a long, grinding ring. Corporal Sam Brodkin, the orderly, answered. "Yes, sir. Yes, sir. I'll tell him sir." He replaced the black instrument in its brown leather case.

"Captain, that was Colonel Woods from the Inspector General's office. He sounded mean and mad as hell. He wants you to report to him ASAP."

A call from the IG was never welcomed. An angry summons was even more worrisome. I hopped into my jeep and high-tailed it to the IG's office.

Lieutenant Colonel Randolph Woods was a native of Arkansas. Before the war, he had served as a Captain in the army for about two years. Later, he slipped into the Reserves for no other reason than to hold onto his military title and impress his smalltown cronies. Over the years he dutifully attended the required meetings and visited military camps. By satisfying these obligations and with the passage of time, he was able to finagle automatic promotions. He was recalled to active duty in 1941 as a Lieutenant Colonel. Because of his legal background, he was assigned to the Inspector General's Department.

Colonel Woods sat behind a long table that served as his desk. It was covered with scattered documents and various office knickknacks. An overfull ashtray with the stub of a cigar on a heap of ash sat at his elbow. The surrounding office area was as messy as his desk, but then, so was he. He was unkempt and a pound or two short of being classified overweight, barely able to squeeze into his uniform.

"Captain D'Amore, reporting as ordered, sir!" I snapped the words when I entered the office.

"Captain," the colonel barked, "Your sorry ass is in hot water, *real* hot water! In fact, you are a likely candidate for a court martial!"

Staggered by the blunt condemnation, I was barely able to say, "Colonel, I have no idea what you are talking about."

"Well, let me tell you what I'm talking about," the colonel shouted as he pushed a few papers aside and picked up a notepad. "I have been given a long list of complaints about your actions as a commander. First, it is said that you harassed your men and subjected them to undue and prolonged training exercises; that you confiscated and destroyed, by burning, personal property that belonged to the men; that aboard the ship you continued to subject your men, seasick or not, to confinement under the guise of schooling; that you tagged an additional seven-day restriction onto an official one that had just been completed; and on an on!" His litany complete, he hoisted his large frame out of his chair and bellowed out, "*Are these claims even halfway true?*"

"Somewhat," I began to answer, "But . . . "

Before I could elaborate, the colonel broke in with a killing stab, "Well, I'll be hornswoggled, tickled pink, and dipped in pig shit! Looks like you did everything but slap a soldier. Who the hell do you think you are? Patton?"

Overstepping his bounds, the colonel extended his rage, using damnable words. It looked as though he had already jumped to a conclusion, whereas his duty was only to consider, with fairness, any and all complaints and allegations concerning conditions detrimental to the service, *not to arbitrarily pass judgment on them.*

"May I say something that will clear things up?" I tried to sound composed, contrary to the roiling scare that was building within me.

"Certainly. We don't hang anyone until the noose is in place." The colonel whooshed.

"First, may I use your phone?" The question was made with a controlled, offhanded tone.

"Go ahead." He appeared to be taken back by the request and answered with an indifferent wave of his hand.

"Sam," I said, as calmly as possible, into the field phone, "Please gather your morning report files and get my briefcase. Bring them to the IG's office. Tell Lieutenant Newlin and Lieutenant Gillespie to come along. And, Sam, hurry."

Before being drafted into military service, Sam Brodkin owned and operated a "mom and pop" grocery in Brooklyn, New York. He was thirty-six years old, short, and rotund. As any successful storekeeper should be, he was exact and detailed in everything he did. He brought those attributes with him to the transportation company. Honoring them, he was appointed to act as the company orderly.

Apparently, the colonel was taken in by the faked nonchalance. For a long while, he just stared, then abruptly retrieved the stub of his cigar from the ash heap, jammed it in his mouth, irritably clenched it between his teeth and stomped over to the lone window behind the makeshift desk. Shortly after his crotchety show, the two lieutenants and the orderly arrived. Perfunctory introductions were preformed, and the meeting began.

"Gentlemen, the colonel scolded me in an accusatory and uncompromising way the past half hour. It's apparent he received a cock-and-bull story from one of our men. I want to give the colonel the public record and facts about our company, and want you three to cut in any time you feel that what I say is exaggerated, incorrect, or even one bit off base."

I began by describing the manner and condition by which the company was formed and that, in spite of the known shortage of equipment and the horrendous malassignments, it had been earmarked as a participant in the early stages of the European operations.

Listening to the descriptive account, the colonel didn't appear to be persuaded. His scowls and lopsided grimaces reflected a growing position of doubt. It looked like he was not about to accept the fact that army administrators would saddle a new company commander with untrained soldiers and with such a responsibility. Noticing the reaction, Newlin and Gillespie, in turn, jumped in to corroborate the lengthy account, then Brodkin followed up by giving the colonel a copy of the military occupational specialties required to perform related tasks, highlighting that, previous to training, most of the men were not qualified to effect them.

"Well, now," the colonel drawled, "what you say and present sounds powerful and *appears* to be worthy of belief, but then, why wouldn't you guys lay it on thick? The four of you may have dreamed up a shocking situation because of the *so-called* malassginments. To me it sounds like nothing more than a 'save-your-ass assessment' of the situation."

Digging into my briefcase, I pulled out a copy of the letter written to the Commanding General, along with a copy of the reply, and handed both to the colonel. "I trust you will accept the assessment of these gentlemen and their acknowledgement of the malassignments."

After reading the letter, the colonel said nothing. He put down his cigar and made a gesture of obeisance by throwing his hands up into the air, signaling his surrender. Shortly after, the confrontation ended.

Later, the malcontent who caused the ugly interview was transferred, without any request or input from me. Apparently, Colonel Woods took it upon himself to try and balance the scale of justice, quietly admitting that through his superficial review and hasty and faulty conclusion, he damn near botched the career of a young company commander. Still the incident was made a matter of record, which, in part, stated:

> It is clear that certain army conformities were skirted. However, because of the nature of the order, the timing and untrained personnel it was reasonable for the commander to take certain actions *for the good of the service. It is the duty for a commander to make such timely and befitting decisions when the state of affairs makes clear and urgent demands.*

When the noncensurable review was made public, the windfall brought on a sudden and positive change among the ranks.

Having lost its position for the D-Day invasion, the company had been given a new status and mission. Throughout the next several months, it moved cargo and personnel between ports and installations, day and night, every day. The only guarded concern that shadowed the missions was a possible hit from Hitler's new weapon, the pilotless V-1 flying bomb. The rocket, dubbed "Buzz Bomb," was loaded with heavy explosives that caused considerable damage in a confined area. Over eight thousand of them had been aimed at London. Most were shot down. However, about two thousand did hit the London area. Although the strikes were scattered, troops and convoys did suffer setbacks from their punishing hits.

The Allied armies continued to race toward the Rhine. They pushed fast and deep. Ironically, the spectacular advance created its own serious roadblock—it outran the link of logistical support. All maintenance, supply, and transportation units on the European Continent and in England labored around the clock to fill the voids. By August 1944, the situation was fairly stabilized, with the Allies poised on Germany's doorstep. There was belief among the leaders that the brunt of the war was passed.

At that point, Field Marshal Bernard Montgomery, Commander of the British 21st Army group, proposed a plan to hasten and bring on total victory before the end of the year. It was code-named *Market-Garden*. The hyphenated-title plan was designed to employ two distinct operations and called for 35,000 men to be airlifted from 24 airfields into Holland, 300 miles behind enemy lines.

"Market" dealt with the airborne element. It called for the American 101st and 82nd Airborne Divisions, with parachute and glider landings, to take the bridges at Eindhoven and Nijmegen. At the same time, it called for the British 1st Airborne Division to take the bridge at Arnhem.

"Garden" dealt with the ground force operation. The overall objective was to secure six crucial bridges across the river Maas, Waal, and the Lower Rhine, thereby permitting an armored advance into north Germany before the onset of winter.

From its inception, many officers ranked the plan as ambitious, especially General Omar Bradley, who had deep misgivings and made those thoughts known to General Dwight Eisenhower. After much thought Eisenhower sided with Montgomery, and the plan was put into motion and launched on 17 September 1944. The ensuing combat continued for nine days. Some phases were successfully carried out, others were thwarted and ill-fated. From the results, it was obvious that the Germans knew of the impending assault, stood in waiting and counterattacked, forcing the Allies to withdraw. The Allied losses were heavy. The British 1st Airborne lost over 8,000 men. The 101st Airborne lost 750, and 2,100 were injured. General Bradley fittingly said the operation brought on an *irrevocable logistical loss to the Allies.*

Exactly three months later, 16 December 1944, the Germans surprised the Allied forces when they employed eight Panzer divisions and thirteen Infantry divisions to push through the Ardennes in a bid to recapture the city of Antwerp, Belgium. The Allies were caught off guard. Supplies of gas, oil, and ammo, already low, were drained. Troop and logistical support were desperately needed. Air support was impossible at the time because of bad weather conditions.

The Commander of the IX Troop Carrier Wing gave a situation report to all unit commanders within the field of logistics. The rundown was based on the superficial, but critical, information on hand.

"Gentlemen, as you know, our forces have been pushing on and advanced rapidly through northern France. A couple of months ago, early September, we were in Holland poised along the north end of Germany's western fortification, the Siegfried Line. At the same time, the British forces were firmly set in Brussels and Antwerp. Everyone marveled at the progress and our posture, and predicted total victory before Christmas.

"Sadly, we are stymied because our logistical posture has been severely weakened, primarily because our troops already had overrun the supply line, and the drain caused during the operation *Market Garden.* Making matters worse, poor weather conditions continue to prevent resupply by air. Right now, the only way to feed the supply pipeline is to get the goods up there by truck from Normandy . . . and you know that's a four hundred mile run. Apparently, the Germans recognized our predicament and took advantage of the situation. They started a fanatical offensive thrust to the west to regain Antwerp." After a short pause he let out with a chocked voice, "To show how maddening they have become, we just learned that in Malmedy, Belgium, just north of Bastogne, a Nazi command machine-gunned and massacred over seventy of our troops that they held as prisoners of war."

That statement shocked the convened commanders. They broke into a gaggle of furious voices.

"Surely, the Nazis will pay dearly for that infamous behavior. More Allied troops are being sent up north to beef up our forces. Patton and an armored relief column of the U.S. Third Army is already on its way. In the meantime, the Allied Airborne Armies are screaming for supplies and airplane engines and more ammunition. The logistics people and the truck companies on the Continent have had, and still do have, their hands full. They don't have the men to go back and dig out the mountain of ammo and the other prime cargo, including aircraft supplies, that is mired in some damn awful location. The 1st Allied Airborne needs aircraft engines and supplies, now! It looks like the fastest way to get them over there is to have our truck companies deliver them right now." He stopped speaking and, lowering his head, ruffled through the paper notes on the lectern in front of him.

"Sir," I called out. "After delivering the engines and supplies to the Allied Airborne Division in France, why not pick up some of the frustrated cargo and bring it back here, then leapfrog it by air and truck to forward depots. Not only would we salvage some equipment, it would save a lot of time in getting some of those supplies up to the front."

The room became silent for a long *don't-get-involved* moment. No one ventured to concur or oppose such a singular suggestion. The commander momentarily withheld a comment, but he appeared to be considering the idea while staring at me. "Well, damn! That's better than coming back empty. Any of the frustrated cargo that we retrieve will help the logistic units here and over there." Then, he softly poked with, "As a start, would you consider your outfit, the 2249th, ready to undertake such an unpredictable assignment?"

"YESSIR," was the loud, enthusiastic one-word reply.

After a detailed briefing, I raced back to the old shed that served as the company orderly room and rushed in.

"Cliff, Bob! Hey guys, good news! A bunch of us is going to start and assist in a new mission where we may get our asses shot off. Get ready!"

"What gives?" Newlin asked excitedly.

"I'll fill you guys in as we get ready. Cliff, I want you to go along with me on this segment of the mission, First, pick sixty men. Then, get the best maintained twenty-two trucks and my jeep ready to roll. Bob, I want you to stay here with Sam to mind the shop and the rest of the men until we get back in about ten days."

"Heck," Gillespie rolled the word slowly, then said, "I'm kinda jealous that Cliff is getting the chance to go, but I know my mom will be glad that I won't be going where they may shoot my ass off."

Immediately, action was taken to prepare for the departure. Everything was in place by mid-afternoon, including a letter of authority to carry through the mission. That evening, the loaded convoy departed Membury and Greenham Commons, England. It weaved through equipment-chocked English roadways and on to Gossport, the designed port of embarkation. Through English calmness and controlled procedures, the vehicles were loaded onto several Landing Craft Tank (LCT) destined for Le Havre, France. The harbor master made note that the cargo consisted of aircraft engines and parts. Because of the "roll on, roll off" feature of the LCT, the vehicles were on board and secured within one hour. Fortunately, the Channel was as calm as a backyard pond, that permitted the crossing in less than eleven hours, arriving at Le Havre on the morning of 26 December 1944; it took several days via circuitous routes to make most of the deliveries. Afterward, the convoy worked its way, zigzagging and stopping here and there, to pick up and load the frustrated cargo. The bumping, skidding, and stalling of the vehicles on the makeshift roads caused problems and delays. Accidents occurred. Fortunately, the three mechanics on the team were able to accomplish most truck repairs without difficulty. However, on the ninth day, two trucks were damaged beyond the capabilities of the team. To abandon the vehicles was not an option; the potential payload could not be sacrificed.

"Cliff, take the convoy to Omaha Beach and pick up the ammo that's bogged down along the beach area. And Cliff, overload the trucks. Put at least five tons on each. In the meantime, I'll limp these two to a repair depot and hopefully swap them for two good ones. Afterward, we'll meet at Cherbourg to continue on."

An Ordnance depot was located to the north of Orleans. It was spread over one hundred acres and held hundreds of vehicles of all types. Some were deadlined, some were undergoing repair, and others had already been repaired and were ready for service. The scene forced me to believe that it would be easy to rejoin the convoy before the end of the day. After talking with a swaggering major who was in charge of repairs and replacements of the 2 ½-ton cargo trucks, I ended with a plea.

"Major Rudagaire, I'm on a critical mission and must return to my convoy before morning. I'm sure, from what I described, you will agree that my situation calls for priority care and you will agree to get me back on the road right away."

"Can't do, can't do." The major cut in abruptly as he spurted a stream of tobacco juice from between his lips, then started to walk away to attend to other matters.

"Why not?"

"Hey, look around you." The major shouted as he came to an abrupt stop. "I got a yard full of problems here and a pisspot full of 'six bys' that I gotta repair."

"Forget about *repairing* my vehicles. Just swap two good trucks for my two and I'll be on my way."

"Captain, the answer is *No!* It seems like everyone around here is on a critical mission. Anyway, your accident occurred outside my area of responsibility. You better find another depot further south." Pausing, he added, "And do you realize the amount of paperwork that would be involved if I agreed to make the swap?"

With a voice brimming with anger, I shouted, "Major, we are at war! What the hell does geography and pencil and paper have to do with this simple request?"

The major was caught short by the question and accompanying anger. He glared, aimed another stream of tobacco juice at the ground, wiped his hands on his soiled Class A uniform shirt and shot back with a final blast.

"Hey, Captain, I got work to do. Piss off. Don't break my balls." Then, he ordered, "Leave your vehicles and wait your turn, or get going. *So long!*" He took a step to walk away.

"Hey, Major, wait a minute! I do respect your grade and position, but let's end this horseshit! I do have a critical job to do, and if you and I are in the same army, you'd better swap vehicles now or I will see that your balls *are* broken when I report your ass."

I pulled out the letter of authority and shoved it in front of the major, saying, "Now read this."

Nothing more was said. Within an hour, the swap was completed and the two new trucks joined the convoy at Cherbourg. After loading the trucks, the men were served, the only hot meal they had since leaving England, compliments of the 559th Quartermaster Railroad Company.

The next morning, we began our return journey to the port of Le Havre. It became more difficult with each mile. Unlike the initial trip where some good roads permitted a speed up to twenty-five miles an hour, the convoy now had to churn through roads it on its own; at a speed as low as five miles an hour. Adding to this woe was the unforeseen heavy consumption, and resultant shortage, of gas. A resourceful, brash, and conniving sergeant . . . *every outfit had one* . . . was let loose with two other men to scrounge gas from anywhere and in any way thcy could. Upon their triumphant return, no questions were asked. The "requisitioned" supply of gas was siphoned into the dry tanks. The next day, the heavily loaded convoy, with sixty-two exhausted men, limped into the port at Le Havre.

A Landing Ship Tank (LST) was in dock. The letter of authority prompted the harbormaster to assign it for the return trip to England. When the captain of the vessel, an English naval officer, was made aware that more than seventy tons of ammunition was part of the payload, he was anxious to set sail before the forecasted weather hit the port.

"Captain! Please get the trucks that are carrying the ammo on this ship. The others will have to wait and get another ship. Hurry, please. The weather chaps say the waters will become rather nasty within a few hours."

"Yes, sir!" Then addressing Newlin, "Cliff, I'll take care of loading this LST. You get the rest of the vehicles and men on another one."

The exercise was completed in about an hour. The master of the ship held a short meeting and outlined the rules governing all. The he said, "The forecast doesn't sound good. We do experience bad weather on the Channel, but once in a while we get a zinger. The weather chaps say we will sail into one today and definitely hit rough, turbulent waters. Because of that and because of the itchy payload we are carrying, I want everyone to take extraordinary security precautions. There are pre-designated security points topside and below. Captain, you personally, must check those locations at least once every hour."

The men secured the overloaded trucks to the ship's locking devices by running a ribbon of heavy chains around the wheels and axles of each vehicle, then snapping the ends of the chains to the heavy steel eyelets that were part of the original equipment when the bulkheads were manufactured. In the meantime, the sailors secured heavy rope along the deck as a lifeline to hang onto, especially when making the security checks.

The first hour of the crossing was pleasant enough and falsely alluded to an easement in the forecast; the following hour proved otherwise. The Channel became *downright belligerent*! The ship began to rock convulsively from side to side. The successive shunts and double shunts dealt their share of damaging blows that raised the adrenaline level of everyone aboard. Most men became seasick and lost their sea legs. Perhaps because of fear and worry about the trucks and their cargo, I was forced to adjust to the motion of the ship and was able to cope fairly well without becoming ill. On one of the required hourly checks, I visited the master of the vessel who was making an entry in the ship's log.

"Hey, Captain! You look weather-beaten, but for a landlubber, you're holding up quite well . . . actually, from what I hear, a hell of a lot better than most. But don't let your guard down. Be extremely cautious out there. Look what happened here." He pointed to a heavy, three-foot-high steel safe. "That bloody thing broke loose from its bolts and slid from starboard to port, missing me by inches."

"Wow! I didn't realize the force was *that* great."

"It was the constant rocking that loosened the bolts. Frankly, I'm concerned about your trucks. I'd hate to have one of those duckies break lose. Perhaps you should doublecheck the chains, hooking and lashing."

I hurried out of the master's cabin and reached for the makeshift lifeline. Chocking the rope with one hand while alternating with the other, I struggled to pull myself forward along the gangway to get below to the tank deck and the trucks. Intermittently, I was able to slide ahead with a few quick steps, then the wind and rocking motion would force me back a step or two. I became a solo cha-cha artist on the open deck. Suddenly, the ship changed its rhythm. Like a gregarious dolphin, it skimmed the water on its stern with its bow looking heavenward. Then it flopped forward and down, hitting the water with a whack, over and over again. In spite of the jerks, bounces and falls, I was able to find and use a massive come-along, which was stored in the ship's hold, to tighten the chains.

The waters of the Channel continued their merciless pounding all the way to the port at Portsmouth. On that day, 6 January 1945, the trucks and a ragged bunch of sick soldiers hit English soil. The master of the vessel addressed the men, thanking them for the support then added, "Captain, your men could call you Ahab. You did a smashing job and performed as doggedly as he." Then kiddingly, he whispered, "But tell me, didn't you get sick and sneak to the rail to up-chuck just a little bit?"

"Go near the *Rail?* Hell, no! I was too scared."

The cargo was off-loaded at Membury and Greenham Commons and immediately reshipped by air to the forward positions in France.

The battle continued to rage in the woods south of Belgium. German tanks positioned themselves around the key point of Bastogne, which was the vital crossroads for rail and road traffic and essential for any substantive movement. At the time, Bastogne remained in the hands of the Allies with a complement of fourteen thousand American troops. To sustain it, more supplies were needed. All support units on the Continent continued to scramble and rush a transfusion of man, fuel, and ammunition.

On 14 January, just one week after the completion of the first convoy, the commander of the IX Troop Carrier Wing charged me with the command of a composite group of six officers, 131 men, and 64 vehicles, to take on another resupply mission in the Ardennes. As he had done for the first convoy, he gave me discretionary power and authority to accomplish the mission. At the same time, he warned me that a sizable number of Germans soldiers were in the Luxembourg and Belgium area, dressed and posing as American soldiers, while stalking supply convoys as a prime target.

The 2249th cadre led the newly designed and formulated convoy and headed south from Greenham Commons. At Membury, six highly qualified cadres from six other transportation companies hooked on. At that point, the convoy held sixty 2 ½-ton cargo trucks; a mess truck, equipped to produce warm field rations; a wrecker with winch, tools, and a crane; and two jeeps. On the road traveling with a normal interval between vehicles, the 64-vehicle convoy occupied two and one half miles of road space. It was the largest and longest autonomous convoy assembled for duty in a combat zone. It landed in France on 17 January 1945. The fighting in the eastern Ardennes area continued. The convoy went forth to deliver gas, oil, ammunition, and other critical supplies by rumbling through tortuous roads and weaving around demolished buildings, war debris, and wide craters. Each mile became more difficult to cover because of the waste of war. Vehicles that once were powerful war machines were wrecked and made useless and abandoned to lie in unnatural and freakish positions. Buildings that once stood palatial and lofty were reduced to gnarled heaps of stone and rubble. The scene was scary, and it became more chilling when we realized the entire area was nearly depopulated. The only signs of life came from a sprinkling of children rummaging through the debris, and a scattering of lone and weary women sullenly poking through the rubble. The women gave short and emotionless attention to the convoy. The expression on their faces clearly echoed the thought, *When will this end?* Understandably, they already had endured the invasion, and the presence and actions of the French, English and German soldiers. Now . . . the Americans.

The children acted differently. Unbidden, they fell in with the surrounding influences of the time. Unable to make any comparison with the way they lived, they were able to dismiss their lot in life with a practical air. Seeing the convoy, they left their scrounging in the debris to run along the trucks, chattering and begging with outstretched hands. The men riding the trucks, answered each and every call with treats.

A famous U.S. war correspondent, Ernie Pyle, who had seen the long formation of trucks and witnessed the actions of the men, mentioned the incident in a radio broadcast to the United States, saying in part, "The jeep leading the long and unparalleled convoy in this hectic war zone has the word Freeland painted across its width, right below the windshield." (Millie heard that broadcast at home in Freeland, Pennsylvania.)

From the beginning, the movement of the convoy was difficult. Farther north it became more intense. Negotiating the trucks through the torn-up roads, around craters, and through war debris and snow, made progress slow. During the night, travel became more hazardous. The trucks had to slowly poke along, guided only by the light from the three-inch-long open slits that were cut into the blackened covers pasted onto the headlamps.

Ten jarring days later, it was time to run the vehicles through a second echelon of maintenance. Fifty new tires replaced those that were worn and damaged and three thousand gallons of gasoline were pumped into the near-empty tanks. At that point, in order to speed the delivery to other areas, the convoy was split in two.

"Cliff, take two officers, fifty men and the trucks that are carrying engine parts and oil to Brussels. Don't come back empty. After you unload, pick up the glider repairables. Also, check for and load the nylon tow ropes dropped by the C-47 Dakotas during *Market-Garden.* The Burtonwood depot back home needs that stuff. While you are doing that, the rest of us will push on to Antwerp. Afterward, seven days from today, we will rendezvous at Airstrip A-56 for the remaining leg of our run. And, Cliff, watch out for German soldiers that are roaming around and posing as Americans."

At that point, Sergeant Matt Reardon and I left the convoy to map out an easy route to Antwerp. Late that day we came upon three men crowded into the doorway of a badly damaged building. Two were holding the third, who wore the uniform of an American soldier, at bay with a rifle jammed against his belly. The two captors wore traces of a French uniform. When the man in American uniform saw the jeep approaching, he screamed, "Help me! Please help me!" Reardon pulled up to where the soldiers were standing.

"What's going on here soldier?" I inquired as I hopped out of the jeep.

"Captain, these guys beat me up and won't let me go!" he blurted. "They say I'm a German masquerading in a G.I. uniform!"

With elementary high school French, I asked the Frenchmen why they were holding the man at gunpoint. Excitedly, with jumbled jargon they made it known that several impostors were apprehended in that sector the day before and they were certain they now held another, and intended to treat him as a German prisoner.

Recalling the warning I was given before departing England, my approach became more guarded.

"Let me have your dog tags, mister." With them in hand, I asked the hostage three rapid fire questions: "What is your blood type? What is your religion? What is your serial number?"

All three answers corresponded with the dog tags. Of course, any impostor worthy of taking on the role would be prepared to answer such and other elementary questions. So, I continued to size up the man. His uniform was clean and looked new. He was tall, eyes were blue, hair was of a blond shade. Unsure, I bounced the dog tags in my hand while contemplating my next move. The soldier, sensing my uncertainty, became more distraught and fearful.

"Captain, sir, believe me—I am real G.I., a sad sack since boot camp. I am now AWOL from what used to be a small repple-depple down the road. I'm already on their shit list! Captain, believe me, believe me!"

His expression was strictly G.I., calling himself a sad sack, who all American soldiers recognized as the hapless, woebegone, comic strip soldier, and referring to a Replacement Depot as a repple-depple, an acronym that was used by a small number of G.I.s, prompted a real test.

"Okay, mister, if I get you out of this mess, will you eat a *big pile of shit on a shingle for me?*"

"Yes sir! Yes, sir! I eat that chipped beef on toast every morning in camp!" the wayward soldier quickly shouted.

That did it. The French soldiers were relieved of their hostage and placed in the jeep to ride between me and Reardon.

"Thanks, captain! Thanks!" the released hostage wheezed with a sniveling tone.

"Not yet, soldier." A .45 pistol was poking the man's side. "You're not out of the woods yet. We'll run you to

Convoy Officers

Personnel of Convoy in France—14 January 1945

Nose Count—Vehicle Assembly Getting Ready to Cross Channel—14 January 1945

Convoy Disembarking at Le Havre—17 January 1945

Convoy in City of Le Havre—January 1945

where you claim you're from. *If* there is no problem along the way, and *if* there is such a unit, and *if* they recognize you as one of theirs, you're off the hook. If not . . . BAT-A-BOOM!"

Fortunately for the soldier, a mile up the road, we came upon odds and ends of what had been a small mobile depot. The officer in charge identified the man for what he was: A real AWOL sad sack who was saved by agreeing to eat a *pile of shit on a shingle.*

After dropping off the self-proclaimed Sad Sack, Reardon and I continued to reconnoiter the area while mapping an expedient route to Antwerp. Along the way, we ran into a patrol of heavily armed U.S. soldiers that was working its way back to its eastern command. After exchanging easy banter, the patrol continued to head east, we headed northwest.

I was cold and groggy, having gone without sleep for more than thirty-six hours. Reardon drove slowly, steadily, and silently, intent on missing the potholes along the makeshift arterial passage that had been churned up and gutted into a slushy mess. Fortunately, a short while later, the jeep *did* hit a deep hole that joggled me to consciousness. Unfocused for that second, I shouted, "Matt, stop! Dammit, stop!"

"What's the matter, Captain?" Reardon asked as he stomped on the brake to bring the jeep to an abrupt halt.

"*What's the matter?* Don't you see that train crossing our way?"

"Captain, I don't see any train," Reardon said as he swiveled his head to the right and to the left.

More alert now, I hopped out of the jeep and slowly walked about fifty yards farther north, looking deeper into the surrounding area for the train I had imagined. Bewildered by its absence, I stood in place like a retriever with all senses alert, waiting for a command. Having seen nothing untoward in the surrounding wooded area, I headed back to the jeep. It was then that the mirage of the moving train had to be accepted as a timely predestined godsend, because it was then when I heard muffled voices uttering a few words in German, signaling the presence of a nearby pocket of German soldiers. I wasted no time in rejoining Reardon. The two of us, fittingly, sneaked quietly back, caught up with the U.S. patrol, and passed on to its leader what lay ahead. The patrol immediately went on the hunt. Not long after a volley spat from U.S. M-1 rifles. The patrol returned: mission accomplished.

Now that we held a superficial, though practical sketch of a viable route to Antwerp, we caught up with our section of the convoy and resumed our march westward. Moving along, for the following six days, we continued to distribute the needed supplies. On the seventh day, the split convoy was reunited, as planned, at Airstrip A-56.

By the end of January 1945, the heavy and intense fighting in the southwestern section of the Ardennes area diminished sharply, and so did the need of urgent resupply.

Now, our prime duty was centered on recovering reparable items while we headed back southwest to Le Havre. For the first time in three weeks, civilians, who were rarely seen previously, came rushing out of their homes and hiding places to greet the men in the convoy. The adults gathered while the children begged. I gave permission to the mess sergeant to prepare and serve hot G.I. meals to the crowd. Immediately, the atmosphere changed, resembling that of a huge, happy family reunion. Everyone was embraced, hugged, and kissed. The civilians acted as though the war was over. I warned them that the battle in that section of the Ardennes was over, but the war still raged on while our troops were chasing the retreating Germans eastward.

The convoy completed its assigned mission. On 11 February 1945, twenty-five days from its start, it returned to its home station in England. At that point, each truck had clocked over *1,500 miles, for a cumulative total of 100,000 miles, most of it in a combat zone.* During a "current events" briefing, the Commander of the Wing included these words:

"As you well know, our Allied forces took a hammering in the Ardennes. Fortunately, with the help of Patton's armored relief column, things changed. It took three weeks to turn the tide and win the battle. Unfortunately and sadly, we lost nineteen thousand of our men.

"During the battle, re-supply of gas, engines and ammo became paramount. Our service units in the entire wing pitched in to augment the logistic forces on the Continent. Noteworthy support was made by a composite team from this command that left here with seven officers, one hundred thirty-one men, and sixty-four vehicles, all under the command of Captain D'Amore. The team operated in the combat zone, much of it in the Ardennes, *for twenty-five days.* When the mission was completed, he came back with six officers, one hundred thirty-one men, and sixty-four vehicles.

"The war isn't over. Our forces continue to push eastward into Germany. The need for re-supply is still paramount. Because of that, it is thought best to move some of our service units into the depots in France. Some units will move immediately."

After being honored with a unit citation, and in less than ten months from the time it initially landed in England, the 2249th Transportation Company crossed the

Channel for the fifth time. It pitched tents in the village of Melun, a short distance from the heart of Paris. The demand to distribute supplies had not slackened. The company was kept extremely busy.

On 7 March, the Allies entered and captured the city of Cologne. The 9th Armored Division then took the Lundendorff Bridge at Remagen. The bold and bloody actions opened a road into the Rhineland, permitting the American, British, and Canadian forces to press eastward. In the meantime, the Russian forces pressed westward. The German forces were being squashed in the center.

Rumors began to fly that Germany proffered peace terms. The rumors were tempered when the sad word was received that President Roosevelt died on 12 April 1945. A month later, it was learned that Hitler committed suicide.

On 7 May 1945, Germany signed the instrument of unconditional surrender, which was ratified on 9 May 1945. Victory in Europe (V-E) was absolute and complete. From that momentous day, duty in France was more like a rest and recuperation center.

All field personnel chucked the yoke of "Yes Sir; No Sir; I don't know Sir" regimen. *Not so for the desk jockeys!*

It's generally true that after all skirmishes, battles, and wars, the administrators begin to ride high. True to form in this case, they started to deal out reports and questionnaires faster than poker cards dealt by a loser. Some of their productions were useful. Most were redundant scuts, idiotic in purpose. It was one of these paper-mill creations that caused, for a short time, a blemish to be entered on my record. It came about when every commanding officer within the wing was required to complete an abbreviated efficiency report on the officers under his command. It was a simple one-page questionnaire that listed five one-word denominations: Character, Honor, Bravery, Loyalty, and Worthiness. Each denomination had to be *rated by a checkmark,* as either Outstanding, Excellent, or Satisfactory. It took me all of two minutes to complete the report for Lieutenant Newlin and Lieutenant Gillespie. Later that same day, I was summoned to the office of Colonel Wordsmith, a member of the Personnel Division.

Colonel Wordsmith sat behind on ornate oak desk, devoid of the usual manuals, plans, and directives generally found on an operations officer's desk. Instead, it held only a stack of the rating questioners. The colonel himself completed the appearance of the rear echelon personnel. His tailor-made gabardine uniform was closet-clean and neatly pressed. It displayed several ribbons of service acknowledgment. He sat erect, with oval-shaped glasses resting on the tip of his nose. His neck stretched upward, bringing into prominence the projection of his Adam's apple. With the pomposity of self-important literati, he began his interview.

"Captain, I have deduced—after review of your 201 file—that you have been somewhat successful as a mustang, a free-wheeler, and a maverick. I *trust* you did not mean to pull any of your shenanigans here and discredit the purpose of the abbreviated officer efficiency report."

"Oh, no, Colonel!" I exclaimed, taken aback and surprised by the imputation.

"If that is so, whatever possessed you to fancifully rate your two officers in the top category of each and every denomination on my newly designed efficiency form?"

"Sir, it was not a fancy. I'll admit that for a short time the form and its questionable intent, threw me for a loop.

Then I went ahead and treated it for its worth. I gave an honest evaluation of my two officers."

"By checking the top bracket for all five attributes?" The colonel scolded with a shout as his Adam's apple jumped up and rested under his chin.

"Yes, you see, in my mind there is no degree between the top and the bottom when judging character, bravery, and so forth. Either one has it or one doesn't."

"That's *your* opinion, Captain! These are five essential attributes an officer must possess and be rated upon. They must be addressed fully and responsibly *by degree!*"

"Sir," I offered dismissively, "with all due respect, as a boy scout I had to demonstrate the five the attributes listed on that form plus seven others that are just as important. Certainly, before being commissioned, I assume the person so honored fully met at least the five called for in the efficiency report, *to the fullest degree.*"

"Enough! Can that sass and cockiness! You really are a maverick! I'll see to it that you are pulled back into line! Now, you are *dismissed!*" While he scolded, his Adam's apple bounced up and down with the rhythm of a playful yo-yo.

Fortunately, when higher authority learned of the report and reviewed it, orders were given to remove it from all files and destroy it, stating, *kindly,* that it was redundant.

I wondered if the army purposely had set out to introduce me to a smattering of its fallible officers. First it was Captain Virgil Muse, the vindictive TAC officer at the Officer Candidate School; then came Captain Josiah Macon, the redneck arrogant administrator; then, Major Rudagaire, the bad-mannered, out-of-touch truck depot officer in France; and now Colonel Wordsmith, the pompous desk-bound personnel officer. *Their type stained the Officer Corps!*

While the war in the European theatre was winding down, the war in Asia and the Pacific raged on. On 19 February 1945, General Harry Schmidt and his 5th Amphibious Corps assaulted the isle of Iwo Jima. That battle raged on for four days before the Marines hoisted the American flag atop Mount Suribachi. Fierce fighting continued until the Japanese were pushed out. Sadly, the victory turned out to be the costliest operation in Marine Corps history. The U.S. suffered over six thousand killed and twenty thousand wounded.

The Japanese became more fanatical when they lost Iwo Jima. They resorted to suicidal operations by ramming their planes into major U.S. targets. On 11 May, a suicide plane dove into U.S. Bunker Hill, a carrier off Okinawa killing four hundred servicemen and putting the ship out of commission. More battles continued and many more Americans lost their lives. The Pacific War was so intense and demanding that support units in Europe were alerted for a transfer to the Pacific theatre. Already some had departed. Arrangements were being made for others to go, including mine. Those arrangements were rescinded when, on 6 August, Lieutenant General Spaatz, the Commanding General of the U.S. Army Strategic Air Forces in the Pacific, gave an order to Colonel Paul W. Tibbets, Jr., Commander of a B-29 from the 509th Composite Group, to drop the uranium bomb on the city of Hiroshima. (Seventy thousand Japanese died as a result.) Three days later, on 9 August, a plutonium bomb was dropped on the city of Nagasaki. On 12 August, the Japanese surrendered. The global war, which had engulfed three continents and forty-six nations, came to an end. It was celebrated with kisses, prayers, tears, liquor, laughter and love.

Veteran combat units were herded together onto a Liberty Ship for a return to the United States. Unlike the trip from the States to Europe, nobody griped about the crowding or the odors pumping out of the ships vents or emanating from the bodies of the excited men. They were grateful to be aboard and gladly accepted all nuisances, *until the ship dropped anchor in the waters of Chesapeake Bay U.S.A.!* On 21 August 1945, when the ship neared Hampton Roads, Old Point Comfort, Virginia, the sight of the famous Chamberlain Hotel brought the men to the highest level of excitement. They became raunchy, bragged about their manhood, and bounced rakish stories back and forth, fantasizing about what they planned to do when they got ashore. But, as morning passed and the day ticked on, the raving passion began to fade. There was no sign of even a *late* debarkation. The men became restless. Equally concerned, I sought the reason for the delay. I got it. The dockworkers had quit for the day! The men were dazed. They felt betrayed and became unwholesomely bitter and gloomy. They damned the system with caustic, mocking curses. It got worse when they saw the bedroom lights of the Chamberlain Hotel click on. Under the stress of emotion, one soldier gave vent to his feelings by throwing loose ship accoutrements overboard. It didn't take long for the others to imitate the act and rid the ship of many articles. I called for order by delivering choice words that only soldiers understood, and stopped what could have become an unruly riot. I covered up their lawless deeds. I did not take any form of disciplinary action. Silently I emphathized with the men. Feeling they were *compelled* to behave outside the bounds of good conduct, as I had done on several occasions, because of the circumstances in which the authorities had placed them.

The following morning the troops debarked. Aside from the noises concomitant with any seaport operation, nothing was heard. No blaring bands, no shouts of greeting, no welcome wagon. The men didn't care. They didn't give a damn. The simply reacted to orders, fell into line for record processing, and the traditional "bend over" and "short arm" physical examination. Finally, they hopped onto some mode of transportation for a separation center and the discharge they longed for.

II

While the ink was drying on the peace documents that ended the world-wide war, the civilian chain of command began to bring to an end the employment of millions of military personnel. At the same frantic pace they indiscriminately began to scrap, sell, or lay to waste many supplies, vehicles, and other military equipment, *much of it at the very spot it stood when the war ended.*

Streamlining and restructuring the forces became a top-ranking undertaking, affecting the professional soldier who already had perceived that his military career would change to satisfy political posturing and desires. Because of political infighting, the program did not run smoothly. Armchair strategists had to be heard and inter-service resentment and pride had to be assuaged. As a result, it took over two years to fully stabilize the state of affairs, not only in the military machine, but also in the country as a whole. The length of time for that process of change might be understandable when taking into consideration the major happenings of its recent past.

When the Japanese attacked us at Pearl Harbor on 7 December 1941, the homefront was thrown into new and different norms. The Congress of the United States had passed the Selective Training and Service Act on October 1941, calling for the conscription into the military service of men between the ages of twenty and thirty-six (later, between eighteen and thirty-six). Over its time, the Act sucked in men and women, whether rich or poor, highly or lesser educated, white or black. It mushroomed the forces to a staggering sixteen million. In the meantime, women left the kitchen for a job in a factory, an aircraft plant, or a shipyard, where they were paid $40.56 a month. The men who had not been drafted into the service also took on jobs foreign to their basic skills. To provide the needed materiel, automobile factories were redesigned to produce military hardware, trucks, and tanks. Shipyards were expanded and modified, capable of building 480 ships a year. At the same time Army engineers recruited carpenters to build army definitive barracks at the speed of one every hour every single day.

All of these conversions and the related traumatic happenings were aimed at supporting our millions of soldiers and sailors.

Finally, the war in Europe ended on 7 May 1945. Of the one million soldiers and sailors that were committed to the European theatre of war, over 180,000 were killed in action and 478,000 were wounded. Three months later, the Japanese surrendered. Peace returned to the United States after 1,342 days of war. At this point, of the sixteen million American soldiers and sailors, approximately three hundred thousand were killed.

These momentous happenings introduced the most thorough change in the civil and military character and conditions in the history and development of the country. The first major change affecting the military department came about in September 1947 when President Harry Truman signed the National Security Act that created the Air Force as a separate service. Stuart Symington was appointed Secretary, Air Force, and Carl A. "Tooey" Spaatz was named the Air Force's Chief of Staff.

To fulfill the mission of the Air Force, Major Air Commands were formed, each charged with specialized support to the strategic and tactical operations.

Lieutenant General Elwood (Pete) Quesada, a tactical air operations expert, was appointed Commander, Tactical Air Command. During World War II, he was the head of the 9th Fighter Command in England. At that time he insisted that soldiers and airmen be equipped with compatible radios so the soldiers on the ground could call in for air strikes. At the same time, he placed forward air observers with divisions on the ground. These moves proved to be a big boost for the Allies during the Battle of the Bulge, especially during the time of the miserable weather.

Tactical Air Command (TAC) established its headquarters at Langley Field, Virginia. Tried and tested personnel were gathered to perform the functions of the staff requirements. In June 1945, I was transferred to the Air Force and was assigned as Chief of Commercial Transportation (TAC).

Under Quesada's leadership, the assigned officers, enlisted men, and civilian employees became infected with enthusiasm and infused with attention that is devoted to a new birth. All administrative arms set out to replace old ways and rules, to promulgate distinguishing Air Force guides. In that area, my task was to compile available material and information that had clear and decisive relevance to all aspects of transportation—air, water, rail, and highway—and to translate its application into a comprehensive manual. One year later, when it was completed, it became the authoritative guide in dealing with matters and details pertaining to all modes of transportation as they affected or related to all subordinated air bases under Tactical Air Command Headquarters.

A year before the completion of my tour with the command, without a previous alert or indication, I was summoned to the office of the Commanding General. The call was received with a wave of uneasiness and anxiety. It's not often that a captain is called out of the blue to meet with a three star general. I could not guess the reason for the summons. What I did know was that the general was a fiery man with a short temper, ready to explode when any member of the staff went amiss. Walking up the stairs to the second floor, the tension rose with each step made down the hallway toward the general's office.

"Come in, Captain. Come in," the general called out when he saw me near the doorway. I entered, stopped in front of his desk, and saluted. "Sit down," the general invited, pointing to a chair next to the desk. He read the uncertainty in my bearing and added in a warm voice, "Relax, D'Amore, relax. Care for a cup of coffee?"

"No, sir. Thank you, sir."

The general became silent and appeared to be mulling a thought. He picked up a paper clip and silently started to straighten it. When that was done, he spoke.

"Captain, what I'm about to say amounts to a request. Actually, under the circumstances, I must admit it will be a favor to me. Let me give you the background." Again, he became silent, slid himself to the back of his chair, and with a business-like tone he said, "Several days ago an ongoing investigation was completed which brought to light serious deficiencies in connection with the operation of the officers' club. The findings found the club in an abysmal shape that called for the sudden dismissal and punishment of the individual involved . . . you will hear more about that later. Anyway, with the Air

Command Headquarters stationed here, we must keep the club fully operational. That's where you come in."

"How is that, sir?"

"Well, when the investigation started to hit the red zone, I asked the base commander to immediately find someone here at Langley to fill the gap until we recruit a replacement and permanent manager. All personnel files that are held at Langley were reviewed. Your record jumped out of the heap. We ran a background check to verify it and learned that as a civilian you had prior experience, not only as the manager of a famous restaurant but also a very successful supper club. So here you are." The general paused for a moment, then said, "Under current policy, I cannot transfer you to the job to run the club, because you were assigned here by Washington to take on specific duties as Chief of Commercial Transportation. So, you see, administratively it's a little touchy to make the change. I'm hoping you will volunteer to help by accepting the job *temporarily.*"

After learning the reason for the summons, I sloughed off my initial fears, relaxed and began to speak firmly and with confidence on a subject I knew quite well.

"Sir, first I want to thank you for considering me for the challenging position. It is true that I have been successful in the catering field. But . . . regrettably, I can't do that here. It would be impossible."

"Why not? What makes it impossible?"

"Sir, as a civilian in a civil community my actions were unrestrained and not questioned, as long as I stayed within the bounds of prevailing laws. All I had to do was establish a sound, economically feasible operation, manage it well enough to meet the demands of the industry, and provide and satisfy the wants and needs of the public. To achieve those goals, I could not permit myself to be influenced by the elite or by any authority. There was no favoritism. Everyone was treated equally and with respect. As a result, I was recognized as the supreme authority. But here," the words dangled for several seconds, "in this military atmosphere, that can't happen." In support of my statement, I immediately added, "Sir, on this base alone, not counting the constant flow of high-powered visiting firemen, we have three generals and a squadron of colonels, all rightfully holding themselves in an authoritative stratum higher than their juniors. How can a mere captain cope with the egos of this barrelful of brass?"

The faint beginnings of a smile began to break on the general's face. The smile turned into a hearty chuckle when I ended the recitation. In a conspiratorial tone, he said, "From what I have gathered from your 201 file, you never had a problem standing up to the brass in the past."

"Sir, at that time we were at war. They needed everyone who wore a uniform, and as a result, they put up with the likes of me. Today, one lousy brass-hat-statement that may, somehow, work its way into my next efficiency report might do me in, but good. If it were not for *that* . . . "

"I gather from what you said that, if you are assured you can act with complete independence, within the guidelines of the club constitution, which is enforced by the board of governors, and be free from interference of *any superior*, you would take the assignment for as long as it takes to make the club solvent and placed on firm footing?"

"Yes, sir."

"Okay, here's what I will do."

He picked up the length of wire that was once a paper clip and began to work it back into its original design. After that was done, he set it aside and outlined a blueprint to satisfy all concerns. After those assurances, I assumed my new duties in high spirits, and set out to face the challenge to undo the misfortunes of the past and bring the club back to its glory. Armed with the stipulation and the badge of ultimate authority, action to modify the character and professional service was begun. The existing forty employees were assigned, reassigned, and shifted, in line with new and specific job descriptions. Those that didn't fit in were discharged, *knowing* that one such case would bring on controversy, *if not a more weighty happening.* It pertained to the chief employee, Walter, the lounge and beverage manager, who also served as head bartender. He was the favorite Bonhomie on the base *and was the General's fair-headed boy.*

"Walter, I know you have been here for many years. I trust you see the need for the many changes I am making."

"Yes suh, I sure do," Walter responded in loud support, more than likely assuming his support and advice was sought after because of his long tenure.

"Well, Walter, in making the changes, I can't find a spot for you. I must let you go. This is your last day."

"What?" Walter choked on the word. With a nervous chuckle, he asked, "Captain, what are you saying, suh?"

"I'm saying you are discharged as of now. *I'm sure you suspect why.* The bookkeeper has your final check. Go see her for it."

"Captain, suh, you is joshing me. You knows you can't do that. I is part of this here club!" Walter bemoaned.

"I'm not what you call joshing. In plain words, you are fired."

When Walter realized that the intent to just discharge him was firm and irrevocable, he became loud and furious.

"You can't do that to me! You is new here and maybe don't knows I is the general's man. Why, I knows him since he was captain. I dun served him his first drink in this here club." He waited a bit for a reaction from me. Not getting one, he shouted, "I is gonna see the general right now! Yes, suh, right now! Then you will see who Walter is around here! *And I ain't gonna see no book-keeper for no check. No sir!*" With that statement, he rushed angrily out of the room.

The reaction was taken with an air of dispassion, as I was convinced that my undertaking was proper and for the betterment of the club. But a "three star" remonstration was anticipated because of that action. Then I would learn if I really did have the ultimate authority in club matters.

Early that evening, while checking the table settings and service stations in and around the dining room, the general walked in and approached me without his usual cordial greeting. *That was my introduction to the anticipated rebuke.*

"Good evening, sir," I greeted, warmly.

"Good evening," came the blunt response. "What's this I hear about Walter?" he demanded abruptly.

"Sir, if you heard that I fired him, it is true. I have sufficient and valid reasons to have done so. I'm sure *he* knows why."

"But do you realize he is a fixture here? He is a heavy favorite of every living general that ever came through here. Hell, he's served here since day one!"

"Well, sir, he has now served his day *done*!"

Angry ripples began to play across the general's cheeks as he clinched his teeth. He went from the knockout count of ten to give me time to reconsider the action against Walter. I didn't budge. Finally, the silence was broken.

"You're the boss," he yielded, then turned and seated himself at his favorite table.

The next day Walter called on the bookkeeper for his check.

The touchy subject was meant to be buried. However, through the wily ways of a gossiper, the story was revealed. After it made its rounds among the members of the club, I was treated as an untouchable—by all ranks.

Immediately, the kitchen was rearranged to better accommodate the chef, six cooks, and twenty waitresses. A savvy steward was appointed to supervise the waitresses and oversee the kitchen operation; a technical sergeant was charged to keep strict accounts of all food items and supplies; the dining room was refurbished to give it a more pleasant and attractive atmosphere; the cocktail bar was placed on a strict cash-only operation, forcing it to answer to an exact wine, beer, and liquor inventory; the lounge was equipped with several coin-operated slot machines that were regulated to give the player a ninety-eight percent return on the gamble; and finally an all-inclusive social program was designed in harmony with correct etiquette and precedence in military affairs.

One year later, holding to the established covenants, the club was running efficiently and effectively. It was time for me to get back into military staff duties, and request a transfer to the newly formed Air Command, which established its headquarters in Anchorage, Alaska. The honorable three star general paved the way for me to get the assignment.

III

The vast area of Alaska, which is comprised of 586,400 square miles, was purchased from Russia in 1867 by Secretary of State William H. Seward for $7,200,000—about two cents per acre. Opponents to the purchase dubbed it "Seward's Folly," and dramatized its remoteness, climate, terrain, and other negatives. The land was neglected. It wasn't until 1912 that Congress made a move to embrace it and establish it as a Territory of the United States. Sadly, after that momentous beginning, little interest was shown to the Territory, until 1915 when an administrative headquarters was established in Anchorage to promote territorial growth. But the glaciers moved faster than the promoters, and little was accomplished.

An awakening of Alaska's true importance dawned about twenty-five years later when, in 1942 Japan staged an attack on Dutch Harbor Naval Base in the Aleutian Islands. Some officials thought it was nothing but a meaningless ploy. Others thought it was prelude to Japan's pushing into the United States. All of that was questionable, but it was an awakening that did spur vigorous action to fortify the Territory. The army command that was located on Richardson Army Base was augmented with additional personnel while a new Major Air Command, to be known as Alaskan Air Command, was created and positioned on Elmendorf Air Force Base. Both major headquarters were designed to hold a permanent position about eight miles north of the thriving city of Anchorage. It was the start of a significant center of operations.

Millie and I arrived in Alaska, September 1949, at the time of its meaningful expansion. We were assigned government quarters on Elmendorf Air Force Base. After converting the skimpy unit into a comfortable home, Millie served her first home-cooked breakfast in Alaska. Within a second after taking the food, I spit it out with a sudden reaction of strong dislike, and begged, "What in the hell is this? It's putrid!"

Millie became alarmed and, disquieted, tasted the food that she had just prepared. She, too, registered distaste. She wrinkled her nose, contorted her face, and shook her head with a pronounced quivering motion to rid herself of the sickening feeling. Then, she said, "Golly, I don't know how this has happened. Just yesterday, I purchased these eggs when I was carousing downtown Anchorage."

Then it hit me. The Alaska farm land did not include chickens. Efforts to raise them within the Interior were made, but yet unsuccessful. The only alternative was cold storage eggs, shipped from Seattle and held in storage for as long as six months! Naturally they carried a "bite," foreign to the taste of the *cheechakos* . . . the newcomers to the land.

Feeling regrettable because of my faultfinding outburst, I'd gently pulled Millie toward me, and with a buzz, said, "Well, honey, yesterday you said you are ready to run into town and get a taste of the local flavor. Golly damn, you did . . . for the both of us."

Ironically, before the two-year tour in Alaska came to an end, we, like the sourdoughs and old-time prospectors, developed a taste for storage eggs. On a return to the

States, we found fault with the taste of "fried eggs, sunny side up." They had to be doctored with a gob of ketchup! (Later, the attempt to raise chickens, Alaska became successful. In the Interior, menus carried the notation, "storage eggs served only by request!")

After assuming the position of Chief of Transportation for the Alaskan Air Command, I was promoted to the grade of Major, Officer Classification: 04. A week later, I teamed up with the logisticians of the Air Command and the Army Command to evaluate the infrastructure and then review the transportation capabilities of the three major water ports of entry, including Valdez, Seward and Whittier. The main purpose was to determine the maximum potential cargo each port would be capable to handle when faced with different emergencies, and also which was most suitable to accept different types of cargo under different circumstances.

The preliminary study had shown that Seward had been widely used for the movement of cargo into the Interior, even though the rail line from the port to a point northwest, for about one hundred miles, was steep and tortuous, which made it impossible for the train to keep on a definite schedule . . . especially during the winter months when the snowfall measured up to twenty feet! These drawbacks could be tolerated and taken in stride during peace time . . . . definitely not adequate to meet extreme emergencies.

Valdez was considered to be a very good port of entry because it was situated only 371 rail miles from Fairbanks, also it was blessed with a road that connected with the Richardson Highway that permitted freight trucks to make a run to Fairbanks in less than fifteen hours . . . most advantageous for use for truck-laden cargo.

Whittier was considered to be the best. It was the easiest and least costly to use. It connected with the Alaska Railroad and permitted rapid movement of cargo into Anchorage and on to Fairbanks, the thriving city built on either side of the winding Chena River.

Armed with the basic data pertaining to the three key ports, our military team joined operations with the civil servant team that was headed by Mister John P. Johnson.

Mister John P. Johnson, a highly respected powerhouse, had been appointed by Secretary of Interior, Harold Ickes, to manage the Alaska Railroad along with the Mount McKinley Park Hotel, both federally funded, built and operated. He was given a free hand to modernize and rehabilitate both entities. From all indications, it was time. Little attention had been given to the railroad from the day it came into being in 1915, followed with a terminal in Seward in 1923.

Johnson wasted no time in accomplishing the related tasks. He employed over two thousand hardy persons, including administrators, engineers, technicians and laborers. The engineers and technicians designed sweeping plans to carve into a mountainside in order to relocate and stabilize segments of the railroad. The changes were many and continued to enhance the operation of the railroad. However, Mother Nature caused occasional and unexpected interruptions. During the winter, it was necessary to clear the tracks as soon as the snow fell. That in itself was not a problem. All leading diesel engines were equipped with a heavy plow that was capable of throwing aside huge drifts of snow. Ironically, it was the cleared tracks that contributed to the interruptions.

Alaska, the home of many species of wildlife, nurtured 150,000 moose, some weighing up to 1,200 pounds.

When the snow made it difficult for a moose to find a feeding ground, it instinctively headed for the cleared track. There, it would walk along the track searching for suitable feeding grounds. Everyone marveled at this intuitive action. Unfortunately, when a moose came to one of the many trestles along the line, its legs would invariably slide between the wooden ties to dangle in the open space below. Because of its size and weight, it was impossible for the moose to remove itself from the trap. Consequently, when the train approached the scene, it had no recourse but to use what the natives dubbed the "Moose Gooser," which was a long, heavy blade attached to a snowplow. At high speed the Gooser would ram into the trapped animal, destroy it, and push it out of the way. It was not only an ugly, gory, and pitiable waste of wildlife, it caused serious delays and operations.

To eliminate the slaughter and the delays, our team came up with a simple solution. Each of the many trestles was modified by installing durable sheeting which covered the wooden cross members, thereby providing the moose with a platform for safe passage. The covering became known as the "moose carpet."

The small and large projects to modernize the railway never ended. High-powered diesel locomotives replaced the steam locomotives. New and comfortable coaches replaced the old passenger cars. All cars and engines were well-appointed and painted blue and gold. New 115-pound steel rails replaced the worn 70-pound rails. The main concern focused on the refinement of the 356-mile rail line from Anchorage to Fairbanks and to laying a new 26-mile line from Fairbanks to Eilson Air Force Base. Funds became critical to finalize the project. Johnson and I pleaded with the Bureau of the Budget in Washington, D.C., to grant a $7,000,000 supplement to continue the program. The money was granted and the project continued. The Secretary of Interior presented me with a letter of commendation for the input and important actions related to the project.

The dynamic activity within the Territory commanded attention from the general public. The mindfulness fomented talk among the politicians to embrace the Territory as the 49th State of the United States. Proponents and opponents in the forty-eight states became very vocal in support of their individual views and positions. The inhabitants of the Territory, especially the old sourdoughs, remained emotionless on the issue.

Mister Bob, my friend, a highly respected, grizzled and leathery Alaskan, who was the proprietor of a saloon and cafe on Kodiak Island, expressed the feelings of most natives.

"Hell, forget statehood for now! After all, it took those big boys in Washington forty-five years to embrace this great land as a Territory. After that, it took another three years before they gave us some paper pushers to come up with plans on how to expand our industries." At that point, Mister Bob exploded, "And until now, they sat on their dead asses for twenty-five years. Now they see the strategic value of this land that sits on top of the world. What opened their eyes? They're scared about the threat that lies in Korea, so now they see fit to rehabilitate and fortify the land!" After venting the sour account of events, he softened his speech as much as any sourdough could under the circumstances and predicted, "Hell, my guess is that it will be ten years down the road before they all get off their dead asses again and give us Statehood!" *He was right! It took ninety-one years from the time it was purchased from Russia in the year of 1867, to June 30, 1958, before Alaska became our 49th state.*

Notwithstanding, the politicians in Washington continued to appoint people to various important-sounding groups and send them off to gather information and make recommendations pertaining to the Territory. Like many fact-finding committees, these ventures turned out to be useless and wasteful undertakings, mainly because most groups carried boondogglers and friends of political hacks who had little or no knowledge or interest about the land, natives, or subject at hand. Worse, most emissaries who made the Alaskan pilgrimage went only as far as Juneau, the capital, where they settled comfortably, like tourists, to gather information for their reports. Certainly, they were in Alaska. But, far, far, far from its heart and real environment. More precisely, the natives that lived in the Interior of the Territory dubbed Juneau and the Southeastern Panhandle as nothing more than a northern extension of Seattle, Washington.

The fact-finding groups that did venture into the heartland of the Territory were laughable. Most often, they arrived with the visions formed by story book tales and pictures. They girded themselves for a journey into a great wasteland which they envisioned to be covered with ice and snow, and traversed and penetrated only by long sleds pulled by a team of six are more dogs. Most definitely, they expected to see villages with round ice igloos populated with fur-clad Eskimos and young children huddled about munching on chunks of salmon.

I had just completed lunch when four persons came tromping through the entryway of Mister Bob's saloon, which was located a short distance from the famed and historical Russian Orthodox Church. The recognizable leader was a middle-aged woman of ample proportions. All four of the group sported citified dress that carried no visible sign of Territorial garb. They were definitely outsiders from the "lower forty-eight" . . . and definitely a new bunch of boondogglers.

Mister Bob immediately took a position behind the counter, thereby signifying that he was the proprietor. The dominant person wasted no time to approach him. She identified herself as Abigail Powers, wife of an important functionary who was stationed in Washington, D.C. and announced, "Sir, I have been appointed and charged with the responsibility to bring back to Washington all significant and interesting particulars as they relate to the Aleutian Islands, especially Kodiak. I have been told that you are the one person from whom I can get vital information for my report about the island. If you don't mind, I would like to ask you a few questions about it and your *fabled* brown bear." She pulled a writing pad from her tote bag as she spoke and readied herself to make notes. Still intent with that task, she casually added, "I must caution you that I must hurry with this because my committee is scheduled to leave for Adak Island in an hour or so." Within a split second of that statement, she began to fire a catalog of fatuous questions.

Mister Bob graciously provided her with the required information in a quiet, respectful manner. When the subject centered on the Kodiak bear, he became bubbling and breezy and talked in great detail about its power and qualities. While he was extolling the virtues of a bear, Abigail Powers, who like most pompous literati find it difficult to accept the word of one thought to be less learned, contorted her face unbecomingly to register skepticism and doubt. In the end, she shifted her rudeness into words.

"I say, Mister Bob, is that bear as huge as you say?" she taunted. "You say it weighs up to two thousand pounds . . . *one ton*? And you say it can yield a fur hide up to eleven feet in length? *Really?* I cannot believe all that, *including* some of the other tales I have heard about the bear and these islands. But I suppose they all do make a good fairy tale for the forlorn Eskimo kids."

Anger flared in the frontiersman's eyes. I knew that no sourdough like Mister Bob would tolerate such flippancy without taking some sort of recourse.

After the self-satisfied Abigail Powers registered her incivilities, she started to walk around the room to survey every niche and touch every rare object that Mister Bob had collected and placed on small shelves to display as prize mementos. Each was identified with name, date, origin, and condition, by a small printed label. A growing state of uneasiness was overtaking Mister Bob as he watched the Washington delegate handle the items clumsily. At one point, she turned abruptly to face Mister Bob and address him. Gasping, she cut off her intended remark when she spied an object standing on a small shelf that was in reach of only Mister Bob.

"Oh," she gushed, "Look at that marvelous piece of *ivory*!" she blurted. "A tusk! Yes! Let me see it," she commanded, thrusting her hand forward.

Mister Bob was caught off guard and stared. With mouth open, he readied himself to answer, then hesitated.

"May I?" Abigail Powers persisted with her domineering command and outstretched hand.

A crafty smile creased Mister Bob's countenance. *I knew the moment had arrived.* Mister Bob turned slowly to oblige the demand. From the shelf he removed the gleaming white item that was about twelve inches long and about two inches in diameter. He peeled off the descriptive label then slowly and gently placed the object in the outstretched cupped hands.

"This is beautiful," Powers purred as she stroked it up and down. "Now this must have been carried by a great animal. I love it," she said as she continued to stroke up and down its length. She looked for confirmation, "Certainly you must agree to that, Mister Bob?"

"Yes Ma'am, sure do," Mister Bob said in a low voice. Then he exacted satisfaction for his previous discomfort by adding, "What you are stroking is the fossilized penis that was carried by a great Kodiak brown bear."

Millie accompanied me on some of my research trips. When possible, during the summer months, we drove the fifty-mile-long road from Anchorage into the heart of Matanuska Valley. The economy of the valley was built on a dairy and truck farms where it produced heads of lettuce as large as basketballs and strawberries as large as plums.

One Sunday afternoon, Millie scanned the wooded grounds for a particular moose that she referred to as *my moose*. The moose did appear, as usual. Spying it, Millie exclaimed, "There it is! Isn't it magnificent! Look at him run!"

It did seem that the moose stayed in waiting for the car. It dashed out of its secluded area to reach us, then loped along the roadway and kept pace with the changing speed of the automobile. Wistfully, Millie whispered, "I wonder if he waits for me as anxiously as I wait for him."

I detected a tinge of boredom in that comment, and knew that she, like all dependents of military personnel in Alaska at the time, had little diversion during the long, isolated two-year tour. Morale boosters were in use, but more had to be invited, to help break the monotony. I made arrangements to book passage on the USS *Funston* and set sail on a ten-day cruise along the Aleutian Chain to Adak Island then back to Whittier.

During the first week of June 1959, Johnson and I conducted a briefing to a distinguished group of dignitaries to apprise them about the rehabilitation program. After official matters were satisfied they, and selected military and civilian personnel, were invited on an informational Alaskan excursion. Millie was among the female guests. The civilian males included Captain (Cap) Austin E. Lathrop, a legendary prospector and wealthy Alaskan businessman.

The excursion started at Anchorage. A new diesel-electric locomotive pulled a modern coach, dining car, business car, and lounge northward to the foot of Mount McKinley, Denali, the "Mountain of the Sun," which rose 20,300 feet above sea level, the largest of all mountains in North America.

Several hours later, while preparing for debarkation at the Mount McKinley Hotel, Millie pressed her face against the window of the passenger car, anxious to view the outdoor scene. A split second later, she drew the attention of all those in coach when she let loose a wild shriek, "Oh, my God!" she exclaimed, pulling herself away from the window.

"Cap" Lathrop, who was close by, rushed to Millie's side and asked, "What's the matter? What's wrong, Missis D'Amore?"

Having been momentarily struck silent with fright, she answered by pointing at the window. Lathrop followed the direction and chuckled when he spotted the large snout of an inquisitive moose pressed against the opposite side of the window.

"Honey, you can now brag to all the *cheechakos* that you are the only one that has ever rubbed noses with a live, wild moose that sported antlers one yard wide!" To lighten her alarm, he added, "Some of the moose along the line anticipate a handout. More than likely, this is one of them that is used to being fed food scraps from the train. Anyway," Lathrop interjected, "as a tribute to the only person I know who has come close enough to rub noses with one of our prized animals, you are hereby awarded a gold nugget!" With that being said, he dug into his pocket and pulled out several gold nuggets, which he had taken from one of his gold mines. He selected a wing-shaped nugget and presented it to her.

My tour of duty in Alaska was coming to an end. Millie was reminiscing then voiced, "Stan, I shall always treasure the wonderful things and sights I've experienced on your tour up here. For me, it would be most memorable if I could fly into the Arctic Circle sometime during this month of June." She added the teaser, "It would be thrilling, to fly into broad daylight at midnight."

I set out to fulfill that dream. A flight was arranged for midnight, 23 June 1950. With my friend, Colonel J.J. Brogger, at the controls, a group of military officers and their wives took off from Anchorage and headed northward to Fairbanks, thence into the bright atmosphere along the Arctic Circle. The adventure was cut short when an incoming radio report stated that the U.N. Security Council was vitally concerned because it appeared that North Korea forces were ready to invade South Korea. Immediately, with that alert, the flight headed back to Anchorage to assume a defensive posture. A week later, on 30 June 1950, U.S. ground forces that were stationed in Japan left for Korea to tend to the military need.

The war in Korea did increase the civilian and military activity in Alaska, but it did not severely impact the way of work or life there. Without a hyperbolic mood, the Army, Navy, an Air Force commands continued to grow larger and stronger.

Our transportation team designed an Emergency Evacuation Plan for Military Dependents. Dry runs were conducted periodically, to fine-tune it and to familiarize all concerned with the governing procedures. On simulated alerts, men, women, and children that were to be evacuated by air were physically assembled on the airfield. After a short briefing, each person actually boarded the aircraft. Afterward, they deplaned and returned to their own personal schedules. The people that were to be evacuated by personal automobile were assembled near the roadway leading to the Richardson Highway. There, mechanics performed maintenance checks and supply personnel stood by ready to provide the needed fuel, medical supplies, road maps, blankets, and other necessities. After the exercise, they, too, returned to their own personal schedule. Fortunately, the plan never had to be activated.

I continued to meet and collaborate with Mister Johnson on transportation and specific railroad matters. One day, shortly before my impending transfer to the Pentagon, our conversation settled on the Mount McKinley Hotel.

"Stan, I'm about to leave Alaska and undertake a huge railroad project down in Bogota, Columbia. I know you can't, but I wish that instead of you going to the Pentagon, you could come with me. I am so pleased with all the help you have given me up here. The progress we made is an enormous advancement for the Territory." After a short pause, he sighed and spoke pensively, "Yet, the bean counters in Washington won't consider it to be a complete success because of the hotel problem."

"Why do you say that, Johnny?"

"Why? Well, the boys in D.C. lumped the financial aspects of the Mount McKinley Hotel operations in with the railroad operations. I know a hell of a lot about railroads; I know diddlysquat about hotels. Because of the hotel problems and expenses, the overall budget is being sucked dry making the bottom line look less than favorable."

"How does the hotel create *that problem?* It's open for only a couple of months in the summer for tourists, a few executives, and the railroad workers. After that, it's closed up tight for the rest of the year."

"That's the clincher," Johnson declared. "During the time it is closed, the cold weather produces a damaging coating that clings to the interior walls and to the installed equipment. As a result, it takes my men about a month of hard, expensive work to restore the building to meet required standards for occupancy." He let those words hang, and continued, "If the place could stay open, it would solve the greatest part of the problem, but I can't see how that's possible since we are locked in from the outside world."

Both of us sat silent. Deep in thought, I fidgeted then dared to vocalize an idea. In a pensive, halting voice I offered, "Johnny, maybe it can be made possible, if this crackpot idea that just hit me could be put into motion."

"How's that, Stan?" Johnson turned, looking for a further explanation.

"First, you must casually bounce this idea around with the Army and Air Force brass. It is widely known they are looking for ways to boost morale of the troops and their families. They have started some new programs, but they know there is a need for different outlets. Why not tell them you are willing to help by offering the use of the hotel to the G.I.s and their families and that you will transport those groups, by train, to the hotel, and provide them with room accommodations, minus the amenities of telephone, radio, room service, laundry, maid service . . . *all free of charge.* Also, that you will provide a small skating rink, a short ski slope, and cross-country hiking trails, thereby making it a fun vacation for the G.I.s and their families at *no cost to them.* In turn, the G.I.s would be required to take along with themselves the necessary bed linens, blankets, towels, soap, tissue, and other such items that one would take on an overnight outdoor trip. Also, they would be required to maintain their quarters and provide their own laundry service. Of course, the military brass would be required to provide a simple field kitchen and serve meals G.I.-style, and grant you cash to cover expenses for the heat and utilities."

"Stan, that's remarkable!" Johnson exclaimed in support of the idea. "I like that! Would you help me present it to the Brass?"

"Hey, Johnny, that's right down my alley! Hell, yes!"

The idea was brought to the table of the proper military officials. It was accepted warmly, and plans were implemented to put the program in motion.

The tour of duty in Alaska was coming to a close. I wanted to surprise Millie with another exciting adventure, and arranged passage for the two of us to board the naval vessel USS *President Jackson* for our return to Seattle, Washington. As far as I knew, at that time, Millie would be the only female aboard. To help justify the booking, I agreed to act as a member of the ship's staff, to supplement and assist the permanent staff, under direct supervision of the Commanding Officer of the ship.

Before departing Alaska on 4 September 1951, the G.I. Hotel-Morale program began to take shape.

IV

On 10 October 1951, I reported for duty at the Pentagon in Washington, D.C. and was assigned to the Directorate of Transportation as Chief, Commercial Transportation. Like all newcomers, I was escorted on a tour throughout the world-famous five-sided building. The orientation tour was designed to familiarize all of us with the unique traffic patterns within and around the spacious corridors that circumscribed the building. Along the way, it was hard to accept the fact that over 35,000 people were employed in the existing offices. The only initial hint that one could have had was the jam-packed parking lot that held over 10,000 vehicles on any given workday.

It was natural to surmise that a profusion of Army, Navy, and Air Force officers, clothed in their service uniforms, would be seen marching in and out of offices within the Pentagon. That was not a factual presumption. Instead, a flood of civil servants wearing traditional business suits moved around just as they would in a commercial corporate structure. They appeared to outnumber the military personnel, and by their demeanor, appeared to overpower them. That air of confidence and belonging was amplified by the anxiety and uneasiness flowing from the newly assigned and temporarily inexperienced military counterparts. The cause for that weighty edge boiled down to a matter of tenure.

The length of a *military* tour of duty at any one location rarely exceeded four consecutive years. It was difficult to find an exception to that policy at the Pentagon. On the other hand, it was difficult to find a bureaucrat or civil servant who was not on duty in that building from the day it was constructed in January 1943! Naturally, such a long entrenchment bred confidence, advancement in grade, and authority, which in turn disposed certain members of that in-crowd to resist changing their old policies. And, they felt comfortable and safe! The system made it difficult for anyone to replace or, even, admonish them. Fortunately, most civilian bureaucrats and military personnel, of all ranks and positions, did strive to relate and appreciate each other's routines.

Unfortunately, it appeared that some of the uncaring, non-elective government officials had no sentient feeling for the military posture. They were inattentive to current needs and managed to modify set procedures and demands to suit their personal likes and notions. Their selfish acts not only bred the growth of an indiscriminate stymie to healthy progress, they also contributed to the insidious belief that teamwork was nothing more than a myth. I got a peek at that disposition of characters soon after Millie and I moved into a sprawling housing complex that was situated along the main artery from southern points into city of Washington, D.C. Military personnel and the civilian servants occupied the greater part of it, but the complex lacked the spirit of togetherness and warmth shown on a military post.

Shortly after settling in, I became engaged in a beer-drinking chat with a neighbor named Phil Kelman.

Kelman embodied the free-spirited characteristics of the time and was disposed to overcolor his usefulness and importance. He was a compulsive fault-finder and always stood ready to recite his solution to any given problem, civic or personal. Shortly after his arrival in Washington, as a brand new lawyer, he was appointed by an influential politician to act as chief counsel for a powerful congressional committee that dealt with military matters. His official duty was to advise members of the committee in legal matters as they pertained to the subject of the day.

"Stan, I saw you lugging a stack of files when you got in last night. Are you bucking for a promotion?" Kelman kidded.

"Yeah, I wish. Actually, I am putting together some material for a presentation my boss will be making up on the Hill."

"Who is your boss, Stan?"

"General Trooper Tedder," I answered.

"Him!" Kelman snapped, an edge of contempt coloring the word.

"You know him, Phil?"

"Not personally. He appeared before our committee a couple of months ago." Kelman took a swig of beer and said, "Anyway, that General Cooper, Pooper, Dupper, or whatever he is called, expected us to bow when he arrived in a uniform that sported ribbons from his shoulder half way down his chest." With a half-smile of self-satisfaction he nodded his head rapidly and continued, with a smarmy tone, "Yeah man, did he have a hell of a time to sell his pitch. With my input, he was really roasted before he got some of what he was after."

"Was his presentation that far out of line?" I probed.

"Truthfully, I can't say that. All I know is that, on the spot, I took issue with whatever he preached. I don't know why." He took another swig of beer and murmured offhandedly, "Maybe it was because of the way he wore his uniform bedecked with all those ribbons and decorations."

"Why should that bother you? He wears a uniform. I wear a uniform. You and your cohorts wear a three-piece suit, starched shirt, a tie, flashy tie pins, and badges. Phil, we all wear the prescribed dress of the day."

"That is so, but it is the vainglorious attitude that some of the military brass act out when in uniform. They demand more, more, and more. Hell, they can't do or get everything they want! They seem to forget they are governed by our laws, and the constitutional guarantee of civilian control over the military."

"Phil, they know that . . . and they do abide by civilian direction."

"Yeah?" he grunted, "But they try hard to circumvent it. Remember General McArthur?" He added with a note of sulky truculence.

"I sure do," I said in an awed undertone. Then I needled with, "Isn't he one of our great military leaders who showed the rare ability to command and win wars? And isn't he the soldier who wore the uniform for more than fifty years—ready to go to war, and ready to die, when and where the need arose?"

"Stan, I'm sorry. You're right," Kelman acknowledged weakly. Then to support the cause of his causticity, he added, "Anyway, a good deal of my job rests with rebuttals. I must protect the committee's position. When we get involved in a sensitive issue, my operative word leans toward *no.*"

That admission revealed a smug and conniving mindset (held by many political appointees) that prompted me to say, "Phil, let me paraphrase a statement that was made by President George Washington to his staff.

"Do not suffer your good nature when application is made, to say no when you ought to say yes. Remember that it is a public not a private cause that is to be injured or benefited by your choice."

After that, the conversation turned as flat as the beer that Kelman held in his glass.

The longer I served in the Pentagon, the more I witnessed guarded snubs toward the military personnel. Civilian servants and congressional appointees dominated important meetings and conferences, giving the impression that military input was downplayed, if not subordinated. To further strengthen the speculation that an image of military prominence was meant to be stunted, some military functions and personnel were removed from the Pentagon and relocated to World War I temporary buildings that were situated along Constitution Avenue downtown Washington. At the same time, the officers were *encouraged* to wear civilian dress, to make the military uniform less conspicuous and lessen the appearance of a military community in the Washington, D.C. area. Whatever the reasons, the military officer felt he was being treated with disdain and indifference.

My belief, that many civil servants treated the military as nothing more than temporary tenants, was further strengthened by an act that was committed one week before my tour at the Pentagon came to a close.

Pursuant to written orders, I presented myself before a State Department official, whose office was located a short distance from mine, for the issuance of a passport.

"Sir," I said, as I handed him a copy of the official order, "as you see, I have been ordered to get a Special Passport because I am to leave for an overseas international staff assignment in Europe."

The official accepted the paper in a cursory, cool manner. He barely glanced at it and set it aside. Then he propped his feet on his desk, exposing a flashy pair of argyle socks, leaned back in his chair and slowly raised his arms, clasping his hands at the back of his head. In a pompous, high-handed manner, he said, "You know, you guys in uniform aren't like State personnel. You don't need a passport, *especially a special one*! Like all other troops, just get on a plane or ship . . . no passport is required."

I was stunned by his shabby and bold remark, and said, "If you don't see it necessary to issue one, I will have to see your superior."

"Go ahead. He's in the back of the room," he replied in an uncaring tone.

I worked my way around several desks, and past people who registered varying degrees of deference, none kindly. When I reached the superior, I was treated with the same strain of indifference, and was told that a Special Passport was generally used for diplomats and was not required for military personnel. At that point, I picked up a nearby telephone and called my superior to report the impasse. Soon after, the attitude and the delay were overcome, albeit more reluctantly than lively, but *only* when the general who issued the order interceded, and demanded that the Special Passport be issued!

After serving for three years and three months, I was a pleased to depart from what I personally considered to be an unwholesome bureaucratic atmosphere, and go on to an assignment where military minds would be more dominant and coactive. When my tour of duty at the Pentagon came to an end, I joined the international military staff with NATO in Naples, Italy.

V

The 683-foot-long luxury liner, SS *Independence*, sliced through the waters on its way to the war-scarred port in the heart of Naples. The slow forward glide brought into focus the scenic magnificence of fabled landmarks nestled in the La Campagna region which stretched from the hill of Vomero to the foreboding outline of Mount Vesuvius. I measured and crowned each with a laudatory tale and pointed each of them to Millie, who stood beside me at the prow of the ship. Engrossed with the legendary sights and warm tales, we were startled by an announcement blasting from the public address system.

"Now hear this! ladies and gentlemen, we have word that, as of this day, the fifteenth of April nineteen fifty-five, a passenger among us, Major D'Amore, is promoted to the prestigious grade of Lieutenant Colonel in the United States Air force. Congratulations, Colonel! We wish you a successful tour of duty with NATO in southern Europe."

Of course, the promotion was known before the ship departed New York, but because the advancement in grade was not yet effective, I wore the insignia of a major, giving no hint about the imminent promotion to anyone on board. Most likely, the information was made public only because a friend pulled a prank by leaking the news to the ship's purser and requested it be announced on the effective date, 15 April 1955, which happened to be the same day the ship arrived in Naples. Among my well-wishers was an elderly gentleman who was returning to Italy to retire in Naples after being employed as a building contractor for forty years in New York City.

The Special Passport that I carried warranted preferential treatment. Accordingly, we were eased through customs, skirted around the crowded port area, and ushered to a lounge on the edge of Via Caracciolo to await the collection of our baggage and further transportation to Hotel Sant'Elmo, an austere collection point for military personnel, which would become our temporary residence.

Via Caracciolo formed a picturesque crescent that stretched out about a mile to Little Fisherman's Port of Mergellina. The scenic setting, beauty, and serenity of the semi-circular road were preserved by the lack of crossroads and automobile traffic. Along the way, a wide, steep embankment, covered with shimmering white stone, created a formidable sustaining barrier that separated the waters of the bay from the elevated roadway. At the bottom of the sloping bulwark, a wide skirt of stacked riprap formed the inland perimeter for the sandy beach that spread into the calm waters of the bay. Fishermen, hunched over, sat here and there on overturned small boats or on the warm sand, absorbed in mending huge fishing nets. Their ladies quietly and capably moved about to help with the tasks at hand. The children, motivated by a sense of duty, followed the patterns of their parents with gay lightness and springy vivacity. The entire scene reflected a disciplined and serene image. In the meantime, a dissimilar character was flooding the adjoining roadway above. Men, women, children, and animals scooted about, unmindful of one another, filling the air with a rumble of jangles. Donkey-drawn carts moved over the cobblestone road with a rhythmic clangor. Children skipped, laughed, leaped and ran, up and down the street with shouts and pranks co-mingling with the constant chatter and vigorous spirit of the passing people. Complementing the scene, a young man was squeezing a soft tune from an accordion for an impassioned singer. All, including, the festooned donkeys, were rackety, unbound, and unreserved. These free and easy actions radiated an aura of noise, music, and romance.

Prior to its unification in 1870, Italy was made up of several autonomous regions. The natives respected their own age-old customs, and spoke the language with their own slant of grammar and pronunciation.

When the regions were welded together to form a modern Italy, the Italians who lived in the upper regions did not readily accept the emotional tone, or the spirit of deportment of those that lived in the southern areas . . . especially those of the Neapolitans, who were looked upon as aimless and lacking sophistication. Despite the antisociality, the Neapolitans continued to act carefree and sidestepped material rewards, steering clear of taxing paths to enjoy the easygoing way of life into which they were born.

A small but meaningful sampling of that attitude and the way they faced life was innocently conveyed during a conversation I overheard between the American passenger who planned to retire in Naples and a white-headed fisherman who was sitting on the riprap that descended to the bay. The subject matter of their friendly discourse wound down. The American, who was about to leave, lifted a package of cigarettes from the pocket of his starched white shirts, tapped one out, placed it between his lips and lit it. "*Ciao, paesano*," he said, as he started to climb the riprap to the street above. He had-n't taken the second step when the fisherman called out, "*Per favore, il mio Americano amico*, maybe you give to me some cigarette?"

The American came to an abrupt stop and turned to face the fisherman. "*Mannaggia!*" Dammit! Have you people no pride or shame? From the minute I got off the ship, all I heard from the men, women, and children was begging and begging. What's wrong with you people?" the American scolded in a voice bordering on hysteria. "Look at you," he continued, "You sit there barefooted, wearing raggedy shorts, no shirt, bumming a cigarette . . . all unbecoming . . . yet you sit there without a care. Look at me," he said, sweeping his arms from his neck downward, calling attention to his evident opulence, "I got all this through hard work! I left this country to find a good life when I was sixteen years old. I went to America and worked for forty years so I could come back here *to go on the beach, sit in the sun, fish all day, relax, and lead a sweet life without worry! You must work, work, work to do it!*" he shouted.

The old fisherman was stunned by the vulgar outburst. He got up, stood on the riprap, faced the American, and spoke in a soft, gentle voice.

"*Ahi, Ahi, mio amico*, you make a biga mistake." Then, with an English-Italian accent he continued to scold, "You give it up the biga *Napolitano* treasure when you make sixteen years, and you leave. *Bene!* Atsa good. But you go to America and you musta work hard for forty years. *Perchè?* Why? So you could comma back here, sit on *marina* in sun . . . fish and fish . . . all full day, stay nice and *calma* and live *la dolce vita sensa* no worry. *Bene!* Good! Good! Siff thatsa how you wanna make to do!" Then with an outward fling of his arms, he said smugly, "I'ma no leave here anna do that alla my life!"

That exchange introduced an insight that suggested that a Neapolitan can endure inconveniences, handicaps, and shortage and still enjoy what he considers to be a full and happy life. It was a helpful perspective for me to use when dealing with the proud natives of southern Europe.

Two days later, I sat at a desk at Headquarters Allied Air Forces Southern Europe (AIRSOUTH), Campo Bagnoli, Naples, Italy to commence the duties of Chief of Transportation for the Southern Air Command of NATO. My principal task was to contribute the transportation requirements and direction for development of the AIRSOUTH Logistics Plan affecting three-member nations: Italy, Greece, and Turkey.

As an International organization, NATO was comparatively new. It was only three years old at that time. The seed for this sphere of collaboration may have started when in 1948, Belgium, Luxembourg, France, England, and the Netherlands joined in a treaty for collaboration in social matters and self-defense. It was probably that action that prompted President Harry Truman to include a supporting statement when he addressed the U.S. Congress, saying:

> "I am sure that the determination of free countries of Europe to protect themselves will be matched by an equal determination on our part to help them."

The seed for the sphere of collaboration was nurtured when East-West tensions hit an all-time high after the Soviets unilaterally blockaded Berlin in 1948.

One year later, April 1949, several weeks before the blockade was lifted, representatives of Belgium, Canada, Denmark, France, Iceland, Italy, Luxembourg, the Netherlands, Norway, Portugal, the United Kingdom, and the

United States signed a treaty bringing each of the twelve nations to the basic principle of collective defense. An armed attack on any one would be deemed an attack on all.

In February 1952, Greece and Turkey joined the original twelve nations. In 1955, West Germany joined, bringing the total to fifteen and making the command of the North Atlantic Treaty Organization (NATO) extend from the North Pole to the Tropic of Cancer, broken into four subordinate commands: Northern, Central, Mediterranean, and Southern.

Those assigned to the various staffs within the Southern Command included Greeks, Italians, Turks, British and Americans. All were freshmen in the new Military Diplomacy Academy, but all, regardless of nationality, assumed and pursued assigned duties with an air of friendship toward the other, each bent on establishing a congenial working relationship marked with fairness and evenhandedness. It wasn't easy. The chain of command was multi-national and new to all. For example, my immediate supervisor was a Greek colonel whose supervisor was a Turkish general whose supervisor was an American general whose supervisor was an American admiral.

Sadly, but very true to life, not all were able to shake off *every* trace of their own national penchants and ways and personal susceptibilities. An elderly Italian captain gave a peek of that when he let his feelings escape when he was introduced to me during a familiarization and introductory tour, which was escorted by an Italian diplomat.

"Hal-low," he welcomed in an overly nice manner, "You comma to live with Eye-tal-yans jewst like you friends who comma here. You, too, maybe take with you somma stuff like Nescafe, somma powder to make-a-milk, anda *refined* rice, too! Atsa good! You wanna make jewst like home. You no wanna live and eat like Eye-tal-yan. Ho-kay! But, maybe somma day you learn how like-a the way we live and maybe you, too, will like."

Taken aback by the scornful greeting, I simply nodded my head in a hurried response and walked on.

"What the hell is the matter with him? A few minutes ago I heard him talk politely with good English," I asked the sponsor in a low, puzzled voice.

Embarrassed by the captain's noxious address, the Italian diplomat lowered his head and tried to make amends for the rudeness. "Well . . . you should know, we still have in Italy what you call . . . " he hesitated, searching for words to continue, " . . . those who think a little like Fascist or Communist. They take offense because they have been told by the radicals that you Americans have much and feel superior to those who have less. Still they are good, harmless people. In time, those few old *fascista* will change and will understand and accept our new designs and related protocol." Then, to further acquit the offender, he added, "Don't forget, Colonello, it is only twelve years that fascism fell in Italy, and it is only ten hard years to this very day, 25 April 1955, that Italy was liberated. It already has been manifested that neither the Italians nor Americans are fully prepared to speak and act diplomatically in the face of this big change."

Long ago, I had concluded that our own bureaucratic oversights contributed to the awkward encounters with other nationals. There were sufficient reasons to blame both, the Department of Defense and the State Department, for the inconsiderate failings exhibited by many representatives they sent to foreign countries. It appeared the two departments either failed to coordinate procedures or just purposely ignored one another. Further, it seemed that the minions of each were imbued by their important-sounding titles, acting free of involvement with the other, and failed to communicate, even in the most basic matters.

As previously pointed out, if a minor matter such as issuing a passport that was directed by a written order took the intervention of a high-ranking general and a high-ranking civilian *right in the Pentagon,* it was easy to see the lack of understanding, instruction, and communication between the two departments. Such shortcomings made it believable that the fledgling emissaries to foreign duty were not adequately schooled about the customs, traditions, and conventions of the societies of the host nations. Because of this overall weakness and lack of judgment, those unschooled innocents took an easy path and divorced themselves from the natives just as soon as they arrived overseas. They established their own secure American ghettos, where they remained, learning little about the culture, environment, natives, or language. More painful still, they unwittingly committed social blunders in a detached manner. They abstained from the use of certain local items, which, in itself, was all right, but they undesigningly showed favor for, and *openly* displayed, their own large supply of American-procured creations, including powdered milk, Nescafe, soft toilet tissue, bottled water, and gallons of Clorox for use to "wash and kill native germ" from produce purchased on the open market. Even the maids who were employed in American households were dumbfounded by the actions of some American women, who shunned the use of a European bathroom fixture, the bidet, and converted it into a chair or a flower pot. Naturally, the natives interpreted these discriminations as a snub to their way of life and, in turn, viewed the Americans as braggadocios. However, in spite of their shortcomings, the American emissaries were eager to serve, although they continued to act immature at diplomacy. At one point, President Eisenhower supported that observation when he said:

> Americans [are] considered immature diplomatically, impulsive, too proud of their strength . . . rude, even his deportment is not admired because of unfortunate incidents on the part of individuals. . . . Each of us, whether bearing a commission from his government or traveling by himself . . . must try to portray America as he believes it in his heart to be.

A more damaging outgrowth of the innocently committed blunders gave the political dissidents and the Communist Party, which gained legal status after the war, the excuse to chide the Americans and the Italian Christian Democratic Party. They reveled in every American misstep. Each indiscretion gave them an opening to use slick guiles, including flattery, free meals, and wine, to invite the benign citizens to a meeting to discuss and accuse the Americans for their misdeeds. The latest and more serious "misdeed" related to the housing program.

Most newcomers who reported for duty with NATO staff, had taken temporary residence in the government subsidized quarters of Hotel Sant'Elmo. At the same time, they were put on their own to search for, and take possession of, a permanent residence for the three-year tour of duty. The search was exhausting for everyone, primarily because of the serious lack of suitable housing. At the same time, it became an embarrassing chase because Americans were unknowingly competing unfairly with the natives who lost their primary homes when Naples took a tremendous pounding during the war, and who were now eager to relocate. The Americans, and Italians latched onto the newer housing as soon as it became available. Most Italians faced a serious disadvantage in the scramble, partly because many of the newly constructed villas rightfully demanded a higher price. The Neapolitans could not always meet that demand. Conversely, the Americans, aided by an additional cost-of-living allowance from the U.S. government, were able to gobble up a new villa as soon as it appeared on the market. Consequently, this condition planted another unfavorable embryo for the vigilant, vulturous muckrackers who had always opposed the presence of a NATO office in Naples.

Within ten days, I was fortunate to rent a sumptuous apartment in a brand new villa atop the hill of Posillipo. The villa faced the Bay of Naples, and presented an eye-popping, theatrical view of the waterfront below and the formidable Mount Vesuvius in the distance. It was huge, with a large living room, an equally large dinning room, two bedrooms, an ultra-modern bathroom, and an ample kitchen. All ceilings were ten feet or more high. All walls were covered with subtly colored plaster and decorative tile. The floors were covered with exquisite Siena marble. Servant quarters, with bedroom, bath, and balcony, were provided to the side of the main living area. The main area was favored with a sweeping balcony overlooking the Bay of Naples. To cap it off, a portiere was on call twenty-four hours a day. Nothing was lacking—except a kitchen stove.

The Navy's Ship Store happened to receive a prototype American electric kitchen range. Hurriedly, I purchased it and had it sent to the villa. A search was initiated to find a qualified electrician to affect the necessary conversion to bring the stove's electrical needs in harmony with the continental electric power. An administrator from the Public Works Department introduced me to a local and popular electrician, who maintained an electronics shop in the heart of Naples. "*Ecco,*" he said, "*Un bravo elettricista. Famoso Direttore, Gino DeJulio.*"

That testimonial was enough for me, Pleased with a *Famoso Direttore*, I drove Gino DeJulio to the villa and showed him the range.

"*Che bellezza!* Beauty! Beauty!" Gino raved, as he affectionately ran the palm of his hand over the top of the range which he circled several times. At the end of the exaltation, Gino was asked if he could convert the local electrical current to accommodate the 220-volt line and the fancy features that were built into the range.

"*Si! Si! Come No!* Why not!" Gino cried out assuredly.

"Are you sure? There are six burners, a broiler, an oven, and lots of wires peeking out of the back."

"What? You no trust Italian electric man? Ma! Donna you know and remember Marconi?" he implored, as he slowly raised his arms and looked heavenward.

Guglielmo Marconi was an illustrious electrical engineer and inventor of a system of wireless telegraphy, but he wasn't here. He died in 1937. Anyway, I set aside all doubts and placed my trust on the renowned *Direttore.*

"Okay, when can you start? Will you start tomorrow?"

"No, no. Not is possible to do tomorrow." Gino was shocked by the implied rush. "Maybe *dopo domani* . . . you know . . . day past tomorrow."

The delay to start the work was accepted, it was assumed that Gino was caught in a whirl of work. Naturally, I settled for *dopo domani.*

Gino arrived on the appointed day . . . in

mid-afternoon. Once again he circled and re-circled the range, muttering time and again, "*Bella. Bella.*" He studied the many colored wires as he hummed and talked to himself pleasantly. An hour later, he called it a day, saying he would return.

"Then you will come tomorrow?" I framed the question as a statement of fact.

"*Ahi*, no! You forget big *Festa Madonna di Piedigrotta.*" Gino answered in disbelief to my presumption.

"But the festival doesn't start until the day after tomorrow."

"*Si! Si!* Now you canna see how fast itsa come here? We must start to make ready fast. *Now!*"

The Italians observe many holidays and feast days to honor the countless saints who are considered supremely good or powerful. The Neapolitan celebrates each with clangorous enthusiasm and a mixture of reverence and levity. In Naples, the queen of all feasts is the Feast of the Madonna di Piedigrotta, a celebration sanctioned for eight days and starting on the seventh day of September. Its veneration is hailed in the usual constrained manner, with a full liturgical ceremony. At the end of the calm and solemn introduction, the spirited people participate in a noisy, showy, merrymaking festival. Barrel organs (*pianini*), drawn by donkeys decorated with hats, ribbons, and ornaments, fill the air with simulated mandolin and guitar music. Young and old alike parade the streets that are brightly lighted with multicolored electric bulbs. The people wear a wide variety of dress. They blow paper horns, wave flags, sing, and swoosh confetti on one another. The parkway pulsates with unbound, boisterous action throughout the day and night. To sustain strength, they huddle around the conveniently placed street stalls (*bancarelle*), to munch on roasted young goat, chicken, puffed pastry, and other delights. When the long eight-day festival staggers to a close, the young are tuckered out, the old are groggy, the donkeys are panting, and the statue of the Madonna continues to wear a smile.

On the ninth day, the day after the celebration ended, I went looking for Gino and found that his store and attached workshop were closed. Thinking like a Neapolitan, I reasoned it was too early. After all, it was only ten in the morning. As I was walking away, I spotted Gino sitting on a bench, talking and laughing with his cronies.

"Hey, Gino, aren't you coming to the villa to hook up the range?" I asked good-naturedly.

"*Ahi, Sor Colonello*, you know I was in big *festa* all time? Many days."

"Yes, but the celebration ended yesterday."

"*Si!*? Its-a-close. But for now, we must rest little-a-bit. I will come to villa *dopo domani.*"

From observation and experience, I accepted that a Neapolitan is not lazy. Rather, each was a good hard worker, *but one that never hurries to, or with, his work.* It would be useless to press the issue, to work *domani* when *dopo domani* would serve just as well.

On the appointed day, Gino arrived at the villa in mid-morning. Again, he paid his respects to the range, then began to unravel the bunch of wires. He became confused. Even with my questionable help, he was unable to interpret the printed English instructions and manage the wires. Finally, he begged his leave, saying he would return the following morning with a chief from the Public Works Department. The following morning the two men arrived, surprisingly, at nine o'clock. The chief electrician aped Gino's respect of the range. He kept uttering, "*Che Bellezza, Che Bellezza.*"

"Can you connect the stove to the Naples electric power?" I asked, with a load of doubt built into the words.

"*Ma si.* Not is *problem.* I do many things with *elettricita.*" Then he went on to elaborate about the electrical jobs with which he had been involved. It was natural for him to do so. Neapolitans feel it is permissible to recite and embellish their accomplishments, especially to the *stranieri* . . . any foreigner.

The two men connected, disconnected, then reconnected the wires in accompaniment to a lot of babble that I could not understand. About three in the afternoon a triumphant cry emanated from Gino.

"*Ecco!* Is all done, *finalmente*! Come, come, *Sor Colonello D'Amore,* we start the stove. *Al'Americana!*"

Elated, I rushed to the kitchen and joined the two electricians. Much pleased, still humming, and full of pride, Gino fiddled with knobs, turning them to start heating up the burners. Two seconds later, he jumped back. All six burners shot up in a flame about a foot high. Neither Gino nor the Chief appeared to be overwhelmed by the outcome. The Chief simply shook his head in disbelief. Gino stood there, silently, in a state of wonderment.

"*Come mai? Come mai?* How be?" the Chief said in a low voice. "*Atsa not right!* Atsa not right for *stufa economica* to make like-a dat."

I learned that this was the very way a Neapolitan dealt with happenings in life . . . things just happen! I gave up. Two days later, I purchased an Italian-made gas range, *stufa a gas,* and had it installed.

To the exclusion of everything, the next three months were devoted to assembling, screening and evaluating all available facts and figures related to the infrastructure of rail, air, highway, and water transportation pertaining to

Italy, Greece, and Turkey. Later, the pertinent elements were designed to fit into, and mesh with, the proposed AIRSOUTH Logistics Plan.

A quasi-ambassadorial team of five officers, including myself, representing Army, Navy, Marine Corps, and Air Force, was composed and given the task to coordinate the proposed plan with the logisticians of the three member nations, Italy, Greece, and Turkey.

Within ten days, the team obtained approval of the plan from Italy and Greece, then it was ready to go on to Istanbul, Turkey, under the leadership of Captain Henry (Hank) Jones, United States Navy.

Captain Jones, soon to be promoted to admiral, was a devotee of the sea for more than twenty-two years. A slight disability put him ashore as an administrator. He was a brilliant officer, reserved and reticent. Above all, he was a strict disciplinarian. Every move, every act, and every expression had to be "by the book," no shenanigans! A disciple of the old school, he faithfully acknowledged and demanded the rights of rank. That predilection was shown when we prepared to board the private and refurbished C-47 airplane for the first leg of the journey. To our surprise, we were given a copy of a seating chart. The captain was to hold the front seat. Behind him, the four colonels were to sit, toward the rear and by *date of seniority.* The most junior officer, Lieutenant Colonel D'Amore, was assigned the last seat toward the tail end of the plane.

On our arrival in Istanbul, we were honored with a princely reception and then booked in the new Istanbul Hilton Hotel for the week. The Turks continued to be exceedingly hospitable and went all out to provide a homey American atmosphere with food and entertainment. In spite of the lavish attention, I was disappointed because every meal consisted of roast beef, mashed potatoes, peas, pie and ice cream. *No native food such as* lamb, goat, goose, shish kabob, kufte, torte, babas, mousaka, dolmathes, or baklava was served. Equally disappointing was the entertainment. All stage shows featured a tap dancer, a songstress, and a magician . . . no belly dancer.

It was natural for the reception committee to think they were providing us with the hometown delights Americans were known to enjoy. Frequently, one member or the other asked how they could be of further service. On one occasion, when I was alone, I was asked if I had an unfulfilled longing.

"Yes, oh yes!" I replied passionately. "I want to learn all I can about your land and folklore. I would like to taste the native food." Then I gushed, "Most of all, right now I would like to see a real belly dancer."

"Oh," exclaimed the diplomat, "How right I was when I told my associates that one could see that you were not only a fantastic soldier, but a sophisticated gentleman of discriminating taste, one who looked for only the best things our country could offer. They all agreed."

I was flattered by the assessment and was about to speak, when the diplomat cut in, suddenly adding, "But, Colonel D'Amore, I am sorry to say that it is not the proper season. It will be sometime next month when the ballet troupe takes to the stage."

I immediately recognized the reason for the misunderstanding, and was about to make my desire more clear when my senses abruptly prompted me to abandon the subject, thereby keeping alive the favorable image with which the diplomats blessed me. To play deeper into that role, I simply closed my eyes and shook my head to register disappointment.

Honoring the well-intentioned compliments of the host nation, and staying within the bounds of the captain's straightlaced, fussy rules caused the mission and related actions to become severely humdrum. Two members of the team covertly shared with me an inclination to break rank, mingle with the natives, and taste the ways of the land. Each, Donald Malone, a Marine colonel, and Juan Nadal, an Army colonel, was a swashbuckling type. Both were men of action, and had distinguished themselves in battle and earned a slew of medals and awards. They were very much alike in character and action.

One evening, after dutifully attending an "*Al' Americana*" dinner and show, the three of us sat in the hotel lounge bemoaning the captain's imposed control. Unexpectantly, my friend, Captain Enrico Cavaliere, an Italian Air Force officer, walked into the room.

"*Ohè*! Stan, *come sta?*" he cried out when he saw me. "What are you doing here?" he asked, as he moved forward briskly.

"Enrico!" I called with equal delight, as we locked into an embrace. "We're part of a team that is here meeting with the Turkish brass. How about you?"

"I just got in from a meeting in Izmir and am on my way home. But, before going back to *Napoli*, I came here to meet *La Mia Carina*, my darling Nadinna. She is here visiting her farther, a Turkish diplomat."

"You rascal. You'll never change." Turning to Nadal and Malone, "Fellows, this is Enrico Cavaliere, who has a Greek *carina*, and now, I learn, a Turkish *carina*."

"Hi, Enrico," Malone greeted Cavaliere. Then jokingly, he asked, "But no American *carina?*"

"*Ahi,* no! No American," Cavaliere blurted. Then feeling that his abrupt utterance might be misconstrued as offensive, he quickly added, "Do not have me wrong. American women are intelligent and beautiful, but they do not rouse me too much. . . . I think they wash away too much sex appeal . . . like French women who splash on much and strong perfumes. For me . . . I like musky women. The more musky, the better." He laughed and said, "So, tonight I am going to taste a little bit of that with my Nadinna."

"Boy, I wish we could go with you and sip some Raki and see a real Turkish belly dancer," I lamented.

"*Perchè no?*" Cavaliere cried out, "Why not? Why not?"

Malone broke in and gave Cavaliere the underlying reason, with a complete rundown of our mission and the related constraints and required obligation.

"*Che peccato!* What a pity!" He exclaimed, "AHI! AHI! AHI! You Americans work too much and never break a rule! Life is to live, laugh, and love!" Then he stated as fact, "Tonight, the three of you must come with me and Nadinna to a proper and private Turkish nightclub, where Nadinna's father is a member."

"I'm game, and ready to break away!" I shot out eagerly. Turning to Malone and Nadal, "How about you guys? Let's go mingle with the natives, eat Turkisk food, and maybe see a real belly dancer!"

"I'm in," Malone said without hesitation.

"Dammit! I would love to, but I can't," moaned Nadal. "You know that tonight I gotta finish my part of the report for the captain. But you guys go." Then with a smile and a naughty tone, he whispered, "When I hit the sack, I'll dream of my own beautiful belly dancer."

"Okay, Rico, looks like Malone and I are your wards for the night. Take us on a Turkish delight!" I called out excitedly, "And you, Nadal, go to bed and dream, dream, dream! But don't squeal on us!"

"I will dream . . . and I won't squeal!" Nadal said with

a smile. "But, you better not do anything that might rile the captain. You know how strict he is."

An hour later, Cavaliere introduced me and Malone to Nadinna Sanal, a Turkish beauty who was employed as an interpreter with the Allied Military Headquarters in Ankara. She manifested a worldwide scope of bearing, having traveled extensively throughout Europe while furthering her scholastic studies. Enrico Cavaliere met her on one of his duty assignments, and won her affection. His manners and charm always worked. It had already paved the way for him to claim a Greek *Carina* in Athens, and now a Turkish *Carina* in Ankara. At the same time, he was engaged to marry a beautiful Italian *Dulcinea,* a sweetheart, in Rome. "Scratch an Italian and you will find a Romantic."

Led by Nadinna, the four of us made our way to the private club. Upon arrival, she displayed an identification card to the doorman, who in turn smiled, bowed, opened the door, and bid us to enter. Within a second, a towering maître d' greeted us. Nadinna looked up to meet his eyes and flashed a coquettish smile that seduced him into smiling back at her. Then, in a low, gentle voice, she recited something to him. Whatever "something" she conveyed caused him to nod his head in understanding and broaden his smile. Cordially, he beckoned us to follow him through the wide foyer.

The foyer contributed an equally warm welcome. The walls, floor and ceiling were covered with solid mahogany, registering wealth and class. From it, a corridor led to the main hall. The room exuded a fragrance of aromatic tobacco and sweet liqueurs. It was dark. Clouds of tobacco smoke that sprayed the room and sprawled along the ceiling dimmed the small amount of artificial light that existed.

Zigzagging around a dozen tables, the genial host ushered us to a prominent spot in front of a slightly elevated platform. A narrow beam of light, the only bright light in the room, focused on three resplendent musicians, who sat near the rear of the platform, dreamily strumming and beating out rhythmic sounds.

Within a minute, like magic, a waiter placed four glasses and a large glass bowl that held a big block of ice on the table. Without a word from anyone, he silently poured a bottle of Raki and other beverages over the ice. Nothing more done or said, he departed as quietly as he arrived.

"That was exemplary and respectful attention," Malone offered, praising the service.

"Yes," Enrico added, "It was brought on by my *bella turko*, who knows the owners. She promised the maître d' that we would pay in American dollars for good service and a good table. The maître d' is happy. He can convert the dollars into Turkish lire for ten times the official rate of exchange." When Malone jerked his head upward in a questioning surprise, Enrico noticed the implied question and concern, then added offhandedly, "Don't worry, it's a Turkish business thing."

Without any real purpose, I turned to look into the room. The lacey veil of pungent tobacco smoke hung over every table. The combination of dim lighting and the veil of smoke, made it difficult to discern a face more than thirty feet away. Then, I shifted my stare to the trio on the platform and focused on the instruments.

"Nadinna, those instruments produce an enchanting sound. They are new to me. What are they called?" I whispered.

"What you see are the three favorites of the Mid-East, especially here and in Armenia and Greece,"

Nadinna said. "The one that looks like a bloated guitar is an Arabian lute called an *oud*. The one shaped like an hourglass is a drum we call a *dumbeg*. The small hand-held thing that resembles a tambourine is called a *def*. Here in Turkey and also in Greece, they are used at just about every festive occasion. Later, Stan, you will hear them strum and beat into a breathtaking, quivering staccato that will send you into a hypnotic state. I'm sure you will sense that when you hear them play for Annidan, Istanbul's most famous beauty and dancer."

Easy chatter continued. Nadinna led most of it as she talked about the folklore and habits and customs of the Turks. In time, the combination of the cozy setting, the low murmurings of the patrons, the sounds from the musical trio, and the concoction of the Raki mixture all brought on an exciting sensation. Suddenly, the dim overhead lights were darkened completely. Loud beating and strumming sounds from the oud, dumbeg and def called for attention. Simultaneously, four variegated beams of light, each from a different direction turned on and blended together to form a small multi-colored circle on the platform, signaling the strumming beat to cease. In that moment of silence, the star of Istanbul glided into the circle of light with a roaring one-word greeting from the audience: *Annidan!*

Annidan wore a cloud of sheer pink veils—seven in all—that hardly hid her magnificent form. With outstretched arms, she unfurled the outer layer and swept it forward with a bow to acknowledge and embrace her admirers. Then with a fluid extension upward, she shook her hands to enliven the tiny bells on the castanets she held. With strong winding moves, she began her dance. It started slowly as she bent and turned in harmony with the oud, dumbeg, and def and the tinkling sounds of the bells. Several minutes took up a faster tempo. Annidan became more animated. Barely perceptible, the musical trio began to quicken its medium beat, goading Annidan to swing her arms more rapidly and wriggle her veil-clad body more expressively. The quivering sounds of the oud became more intense; the beat of the dumbeg more rapid; the shattering of the def more prominent; and the slithering wriggles and sinuous moves of Annidan became more and more provocative. Within ten minutes, as she continued her dance, she seductively and slowly shed one veil, then another and another, until she came to a dramatic stop, seemingly naked. At that split second, the variegated lights were extinguished and Annidan disappeared as magically as she'd appeared. The overhead lights came on, signaling the end of her performance. There were no shouts or whistles. Instead, her audience paid a deep respect and admiration by prolonged loud hand clapping.

"What performance," Malone gushed.

"Yeaaah, she is an erotic, yet innocent dream," I agreed with a sigh. Directly as the word "dream" rolled out, I was struck with an idea that probably had taken root while Annidan danced, but definitely encouraged by the Raki mixture that was freely imbibed. In any case, I outlined a plan to my equally well-disposed fun seekers. From the beginning, it aroused their interest. In the end, it gained their enthusiastic cooperation, and Nadinna was charged with the execution of the main feature. She then approached her friend, the amenable maitre d'. After a short discussion and the proffering of a sizeable reward, she engaged the services of his official ward, Annidan.

Three o'clock in the morning, *violating local custom,* we surreptitiously ushered Annidan into the Istanbul Hilton Hotel. We convened in my room, which, like those occupied by the other members of the team, shared a common balcony that stretched the length of the outer wall of the hotel.

After last-minute instructions, Malone and Cavaliere stepped out onto the balcony. Nadinna, Annidan, and a recruited chambermaid remained in the room. In the meantime, I called the other colonel of our team, then went for broke and called the iron-handed captain. With faked excitement, which left no room or time for questions or comments, I abruptly hung up on both after puffing out, "Meet me on the balcony in front of Nadal's room, and hurry . . . *right away!*"

Like a soldier responding to a mobility alert, the colonel hurried to the balcony. Seconds later, the captain scooted to us, radiating all the signs of worry and anxiety. "What's wrong? What happened?" he babbled excitedly as he slip-slided his way toward us.

I raised my arms over my head and waved for silence. "Gentlemen, first to allay all fears, there is nothing wrong. But, as you may have already figured out, I am a victim of Bacchus, who is to blame for my present high-spirited condition. However, it was one of his Bacchae that aroused me to pull a prank on our teammate, Juan Nadal, who went to bed last night to dream of a beautiful seven-veiled Turkish dancer." Pointing to the inside of Nadal's room, I announced, "Gentlemen, there he is, fast asleep and dreaming of his own beautiful dancer." Motioning for the men to come close to the sliding glass door of Nadal's room, I said, "I invite you to witness the materialization of his dream."

With diffidence and wonder, the two men, along with me and Malone, edged forward to look into the darkened room. Two jaws dropped when the silent tableau began to unveil. Four eyes dilated with rapture when Annidan began to move and raise her arms above her head, gyrating and bending her body. Fascinated, the two guests looked on silently as she let a veil sweep across Nadal's face. When she activated the castanets and broke the silence with the soft sounds of the small bells, she brushed another veil across Nadal's face, which caused him to squirm, snort and roll his head to the side. A minute later she let the veil drop on his face. He swept it aside and propped himself up with his elbows into a tenuous sitting position. His eyes bulged wide open and locked in on the moving form in front of him. The reaction of the two guests was quite different. Aware of the reality, but completely absorbed in the scene, they looked on, amused and slack-jawed, and shifted glances from Annidan to Nadal, who sat on his bed as still as a marble statue. Clearly, he was speechless and spellbound by the vision floating about his room. The enjoyment for the two guests heightened when he unconsciously bunched the dropped veil in his hand and rubbed it on his arm to test if it really had substance. Now, the captain manifested unabashed conviviality, far different from his stern persona. He appeared to be revitalized and enlivened. Annidan continued to move; now wearing only one veil, she stood still, a few inches in front of Nadal, and gave two quick body jerks. At that instant, the chambermaid switched off the night-light. Annidan evaporated into the darkness. I opened the sliding glass door and turned on the overhead light while Malone, the colonel, and the captain rushed into the room, convulsed with laughter.

"Hey, wake up," called the captain, laughing loudly as he shook Nadal's shoulders. "Looks like you had a nice dream. Tell us about it!"

The atmosphere got spooky when Nadal didn't respond, didn't budge, just held that vacant stare . . . until he saw the veil he still had in his hand. He snapped out of his trance. "What the hell is going on?" he blurted.

"She," I said, pointing to Annidan as she was ushered into the room fully clothed.

The next morning, Malone and I walked idly into the hotel dining room. We took a table and woodenly ordered brunch. Before we were served, the colonel, Nadal, and the captain entered the room. When the captain spied us, he bent forward with quick steps and headed for our table.

"Uh-oh . . . here it comes, Don," I said resignedly, "We are about to get fired . . . and on an empty stomach and big head, too."

When the captain reached the table, his face broke into a broad, friendly smile. "Ahoy! Do you two playful pranksters mind if this recharged old fogey joins you?"

Thenceforth, while in Turkey, the conduct of the group changed—dramatically!

After coordinated additions, deletions, and corrections, the logistics section of the war plan was accepted. To a large degree, the early success was due to the manner by which the members of our team conducted the series of actions with the three dissimilar nations. Primarily because, contrary to the expectations of each host nation, no member of the team acted in a haughty or superior manner, nor did anyone exhibit an individuality bent on preserving the logistic demands as originally drafted. Instead, all other national input was accepted with respect and given due credit. In turn, as we went on, each of the three nations telegraphed the feeling that said, "Hey! You Americans are not as cocky, conceited, or lordly as we expected. Thank you for a much-needed plan."

Like all planners, the authors of the logistic plan already had judged it as being clear and complete. However, no plan of that magnitude could be put into effect without testing it to determine if it was clear and complete enough to satisfy all pertinent and national factors. Therefore, it was scheduled to undergo a command-wide "Exercise and Critique."

On 12 September 1957, I received a letter, which stated in part:

> In addition to your normal duties, you have assumed responsibilities for the development of the AIRSOUTH Logistic Plan and logistic participation in Maneuvers and Exercises . . . a noteworthy and distinct achievement for accomplishing the logistic objectives of this headquarters. . . . The numerous meetings required included those with the Air Force Chief of Staff of Greece, Italy and Turkey. . . . The acceptance of the plan by the Chiefs of Staff clearly shows that you displayed unusual diplomatic, organizational and executive ability . . . requested this letter become a part of your official record.
>
> Suat Eraybar
> Brigadier General, Turkish Air Force
> Deputy Chief Of Staff

A short time after the adoption of the plan, the Tri-Chiefs of Staff were honored with a formal dinner-dance held at the Allied Officers Club. All assigned officers attended and wore the traditional dress of their national service. Their ladies wore formal evening dress. The array of dazzling national uniforms and the collection of beautifully styled evening gowns created a striking scene. All evening long, the ladies and gentlemen danced, drank, and laughed in step with military principles and local customs in social matters. They roamed the ballroom and the ancillary lounges, exchanging pleasantries. The ladies favored the large and lavish *Ritirata* for a touch-up and a reposeful retreat. The gentlemen used the small slot machine casino as a relaxing rendezvous. It was at this time and in this room that the proverbial Ugly American struck, tarnishing the elegant setting.

A side door, which separated the casino from a garbage dock, burst open, sending forward an unsteady and shabby civilian. The noise and the sight startled the players in the room. The sound of the machines was cut short. All attention focused on the intruder. The handful of Italian, Greek, and Turkish officers eyed him warily as he walked unsteadily to engage a vacant machine. Quizzically and slowly, they resumed their play. Shortly afterwards, a roar emanated from the inebriated civilian, which overpowered the whirls and clanks of the slot machine reels.

"What the hell is the matter with this frigging machine?" He shouted. "It won't take my money and now it's jammed!" He shook the machine forcefully. "What a piece of crap they have in this guinea joint!" The stranger apparently did not know that the machines would function only with the use of a *gettoni*, a specially designed slug. Nonetheless, with a closed fist he banged the glass cover on the machine until it cracked. As it should have been, the other national officers in the room were astounded and looked to me, quietly signaling, "Hey, colonel, he is one of yours . . . an American . . . qualify him!"

So enjoined, I approached the boisterous, out-of-hand intruder who unquestionably reeked too much of alcohol.

"Sir, I beg your pardon. Are you a member of this club?" I inquired calmly and respectfully.

"Who the hell are you?" the intruder slurred. "No, I am not a member of this chickenshit outfit."

"In that case, I must ask you to leave."

"Frig you!" he shouted. "I'm an American citizen! Who's gonna make me leave?" he bellowed, as he turned to challenge one and all.

It was obvious the Ugly American had to be removed.

"I'll show you who," I said, as I grabbed him by the collar and the seat of his pants, and pushed him along the way, shoving him out the side door onto the dock that was loaded with garbage. All though shuffling, the drunkard let off with offensive language, yelling to all in the room, "Why you stupid jerks, you don't know who you are messing with. I have interviewed kings and queens and many other important people, all far, far above you greasy Turks, Greeks, and Guineas."

Outside, his howling drew the attention of a roving police patrol. After some discussion, I ordered the police to take the man into custody. The day after that incident and the formal dinner-dance, I received a telephone call from the admiral's office.

"Colonel D'Amore," the friendly voice said, "I hear you were involved with an ugly situation last night."

"Yes sir, I was."

"Well, I heard all about it first thing this morning. Afraid that your action against the visiting VIP might be questioned. An Italian, a Greek, and a Turkish officer, came to my office as a group this morning to support and praise the way you nipped the unpleasant situation in the bud." After a short pause, he added, "Incidentally, do you know who it was that you threw into the garbage?"

"No sir. There was no time for introductions."

"Well," the voice chuckled, "he happens to be that big shot famous reporter for *Span* magazine. He dropped in here two days ago, asking if it was all right for him to roam around our command to pick up some background for a short news story about our set-up."

"Oh, golly sir, I didn't. . . . " I began to make some justifiable response for my questionable blunder, but was cut off with another chuckle.

"Colonel, you need not say a thing. Don't worry. I would have reacted just as you did, if protocol would have permitted."

"Thank you, sir."

The thoughts of the embarrassing incident slowly faded away with each duty-filled day. Six weeks later, on my desk was a large envelope, from the Admiral's office, with a two word-note, FOR REMEMBRANCE. In it was the current copy of *Span* magazine. Hurriedly, I riffled through the pages, instinctively searching for any reference to the four letters, NATO. As expected, they popped up in bold type that led to a half page of cleverly slanted facts to make the mission of the Southern Command of NATO sound shallow and questionable. I was not surprised by the tone of the caviling article. I knew reporters were employed to gather and report news, good or bad, about the famous or infamous. Sadly, in that performance certain designing reporters satisfied their selfish interests and skewed their reports to foist their personal beliefs on their readers. And. so it was on this point.

Two months later, military exercises and critiques were conducted to test the soundness of the logistics plan. At that time, appropriate changes were made, in harmony with the valid critical estimates and findings. That finished, urgent demands that plagued the participating authors of the plan were lessened. Although the lightened respite was not without continued duties, it did allow me the time to learn more about the customs and ways of the natives.

One Monday afternoon, I took a seat at one of the luncheon tables in the NATO mess hall. Each table was designed to encourage international dialogue and a strong camaraderie. On this particular afternoon, an American officer took the bulk of the lunch hour to relate an unusual event pertaining to Padre Pio, a Capuchin monk of the Franciscan Order, who in his youth was stigmatized with wounds similar to those of Christ—in his side, his hands, and his feet. From the year 1916, he administered to a faithful flock in a tiny church in the village of San Giovanni Rotundo, which was located on a rocky mountaintop near the city of Bari, a port on the southeast coast of Italy on the Adriatic Sea.

Before going into detail, the storyteller made clear that his account was based on documented information obtained from personnel serving with the World War II Air Command that, at the time, was based in Bari. Then he went on to state that the Bari Air Command learned of a German munitions dump that was located to the north, near the friary of the village of San Giovanni Rotundo. As a result, several bombers were dispatched to destroy the cache. However, when the planes approached the target area, the leader became awe-stricken and frightened by a vision of a monk with arms raised toward heaven, as though to signal the bomber formation to bypass the village. Without any fixed design or order, the bombs were not released on the intended target, which caused considerable discussion and serious consequences for the leader of the bomb formation. After the war, the punished leader drove a jeep to San Giovanni Rotundo to satisfy his apparent hallucination. When he reached the friary at the top of the mountain, he was forced to bring his vehicle to an immediate stop. Standing before him was a Franciscan monk, with arms raised upward, blocking his way. The figure and its stance were identical to the vision he had seen leading the bombing mission. Slowly the monk, Padre Pio, walked to the vehicle and smiled as he spoke, "So, you are the one that was sent to destroy my village." The officer who recited the story ended it by saying, "What I have said about this amazing episode is documented in official records and available for scrutiny."

The story was received by the officers at the table with a mixture of belief and skepticism that gave way to a lengthy discussion. That evening, I broached the story at home, after dinner.

"Millie, I have to recount an amazing story about the Capuchin monk you often talk about. I heard this story during today's lunch hour. I know it will interest you. Let's go out to the balcony. I'll make us a drink and tell you all about it." Comfortably seated, I went on to relate the story about the aborted mission, then said, "Hell, that is so hard to believe. How and why could such a thing happen?"

"My *Doubting Thomas* and Mister *Wonder Why,*" Millie said softly and affectionately. "Always looking for answers. Let me ask you a *why*. Why don't we drive to San Giovanni Rotundo and find out who and why?"

I skillfully and purposely ignored the intended request and steered the conversation to the beauty of the scene before us which stretched out across the Bay of Naples to Vesuvius. Before going into a long discussion, Millie said "Every time I step on this balcony, I look across the bay and trace the slopes of that menacing Mount Vesuvius. It has me spellbound," she sighed. "It looks so peaceful, motionless and reposeful, like nothing more than a huge brown painting pasted against the skyline." She immediately added, sharply, "But I shudder when I think of what it had done when it erupted and buried the city of Pompeii in the year of seventy-nine." A minute later, she softly and hesitantly revealed her yearned-for wanting. "Stan, I was hoping that we could do three things before your tour of duty with NATO ends. First, I would like to go up to the mouth of that Cassandra. Then, I would like to travel south to San Giovanni Rotundo to see Padre Pio, and then I would like to see the Pope up close."

From the time we had arrived in Italy, all our visits and travels were spent on the famous cities and historical sights in, around, and north of Naples. Some of those included: Positano, Sorrento, Capri, Cassino, Rome, Portofino, Santa Margherita, Pisa, Venice and Verona—but nowhere south, not even to Vesuvio . . . it was time. So I said, "Honey, okay. As you know, I have a thirty-day leave coming. First, I must attend a NATO school at Versailles, just outside of Paris. If you like, you may accompany me. While I am at school, you and Eula and Andy Anderson, who are stationed there, can make the rounds in Paris. After that assignment, I am to proceed to Old Sarum, Salisbury, England. If you like, you may accompany me there. While I attend the seminars, you and Jean and Bill Browning, who are on duty in London, can make the rounds. Then, I will take you to Vesuvius, and I'll arrange a trip to San Giovanni Rotundo and on down to Sicily. But getting to see the Pope up close is another thing."

"*Maraviglioso!* Wonderful!" Millie cried out. "You are my wonderful man."

When we planned to visit Mount Vesuvius, we were informed that the ascent beyond the observatory, which was positioned 1,995 feet up the slope, was denied temporarily because of certain maintenance needs, yet Mille had hoped to be able to climb to the peak that stood 4,190 feet above the highway. I solicited the aid of my friend, Enrico Cavaliere the "Bonhomie," to gain permission for a climb to the apex of the volcano. Cavaliere had friends everywhere, and fortunately he knew a principal who tended to the sleeping volcano.

The three of us departed Naples by way of the Napoli-Pompeii autostrada. A few miles ahead, we turned onto the road marked "Vesuvio," and drove up the slope to the observatory. At that point, Cavaliere hopped out of the car and approached the official on duty. With his buoyancy and cheerful disposition, an animated conversation ensued. After some laughter and handshaking, several packs of cigarettes were passed on to the official. Cavaliere then returned to the car wearing a broad, satisfied smile.

"Come, come," he urged. "Leave the car and let's go."

"What's going on, Rico?" I asked, as we got out of the car.

"Just a *Napolitano* thing. *Compaesano a Compaesano* . . . one fellow countryman to another." Anyway, Luigi, the engineer, will give us a lift on the cog-train as far as the track that is under repair will permit. From there, we may climb up to the summit.

So, we rode the cog-train, got off, and started the climb. Cavaliere led the way, Millie followed him, and I brought up the rear. We began to scale the slope, laughing, slipping, and talking. We trudged upward and finished the climb unscathed. At the summit, a cordon of heavy rope restricted further advancement. Millie walked along the roped-off area. She was excited and cried out in a high pitched voice, "Why, this is as tame as any mountaintop at home in Pennsylvania. I'm going to look inside that ill-boding mouth."

Catching Cavaliere off guard, she crawled under the

heavy rope. Edging closer to the rim, she stumbled, lost her footing and began to slide down the loose surface. Frantically, she shouted, "RICO, HOLD ME!!" Cavaliere's hand shot out and grabbed her arm.

When I heard the clatter of dislodged stones, I looked up just as Millie had already slipped knee deep inside the opening of the bowl-shaped crater. Fortunately, Cavaliere kept a firm grip on her arm. I rushed to help. The two of us dragged her back to stable ground.

"What possessed you to go beyond the barrier?" I scolded. "Did you want to become an added exhibit in the Pompeii museum?" Sensing her fear and seeing her wounded expression, I softened my tone and gently added, "I don't know if I should spank your fanny or kiss you."

"Just kiss me, Stan," she begged, as she snuggled her trembling body into my arms.

It didn't take long for Millie to regain her sparkling composure. She began to joke about her being swallowed by the Cassandra. We resumed the reconnoitering but, far, far away from the opening. Later, we dropped Enrico off at Naples and continued with our southbound journey.

As we cruised unhurriedly along a narrow country road, we heard a distant church bell ring out three sharp claps. We knew that was "the first bell," a signal to the parishioners that the early morning religious services would begin within the next fifteen minutes. When we entered the village, the church bells began their second ecclesiastical peal. The tintinnabulation of the swinging bells continued to ebb and swell with a rhythmic chime, urging the latecomers to be seated in the church. Electing to join the parishioners and attend the Mass, we parked our car in a wide parking area, which already held a number of wagons and donkey carts, and joined the sizable number of men, women, and children who hastened to the church.

The peasant women looked alike in expression and dress. All wore a long-sleeved jet-black garment fastened tightly at the neck. Without form, it fell down below mid-calf or all the way down to the ankles. Some carried the Roman Catholic rosary. Some carried a prayer book. Some clutched a paper bag that acted as a purse.

The sight of the American automobile delayed the procession a bit. It attracted the men and dragged them away from their companions. With quiet female indulgence, the women stopped in place momentarily and watched the men with a look of forced tolerance along with scolding chatter. When the men satisfied their curiosity, they made their way to rejoin their companions.

As the group neared the entrance of the church, the women huddled together, chattering, as each reached up a sleeve or poked in the fold of her dress to retrieve a shawl, kerchief, or any bit of cloth to pin to their hair atop the head. This, they felt, was enough to satisfy the rule that required all females to wear a headdress while under the roof of a church. It amused us to see their casual and slightly delicate attempt to please the heavens. That amusement turned to surprise shortly after we entered the church, when, during the celebration of the holy Mass, a young woman exposed a breast to feed a small child she held in her lap. No one paid attention to the act itself, it did, however, invite the neighboring women to coo and comment, well above a whisper, about the actions and beauty of the infant. They continued to carry on with all sorts of good wishes and personal questions while the priest went on to preach. Then, when the priest began to recite the usual homily, it appeared to send an expected signal. Members of the congregation slid back in their pews with ease. Many rummaged in paper sacks to pull out a small hollowed-out loaf of homemade bread that was stuffed with meat, tomatoes, and/or cheese. Unabashed, they ate as they would at a picnic. Others just fidgeted and waited. All of these actions went on while the priest scolded about the same sins he had preached about for the past hundred Sundays. Yet, the people appeared comfortable and within reason for their actions. After all, most of them trudged several miles in the early morning with only a cup of strong espresso for fortification. The entire episode was an expected and accepted village affair.

When the Mass was over, the priest left the altar, exited the church and took a position outside and near the entrance. The parishioners, who had formed a double line, followed him in an orderly fashion. As they stepped outside, the priest greeted each and exchanged bits of quiet conversation. That done, the women clustered in pairs and groups to share a more animated account relating to the local tittle-tattle, and the doings and news, that had come about from the time of their last gathering. In the meantime, some of the men stood by idly, some tended to donkey carts, and some made a return visit to the American automobile. Taken with the friendly and neighborly warmth being exchanged, we watched and lingered until the priest reentered the church. After some mundane chitchat with the natives, we resumed our journey and headed south.

The day became uncomfortably warm. A short respite was in order. We left the thruway and followed a road sign that directed us to a nearby village. The side road was narrow, unpaved and dusty. After a short run, it began to take on an urban style, it was covered firmly and solidly with large, square cobblestone. Then, the village buildings came into sight. The air was still. There was no one in sight. The only hint of a sound came from a large fountain that splashed mellifluous sounds with a rhythmical beat. The scene and spirit prompted Millie to offer, "It looks like we ran into a local holiday. There is no one on the street or near the shops."

I shifted the car into a slow glide, swiveled my head to the right and to the left, and spotted two small girls laughing, shouting and playing as they skipped in and out of tiny coffee shop. "Looks like there is some life over there, I'll pull over and check it out."

When the automobile glided to a stop, the two girls abruptly stopped their scampering, stood in place, silently staring at the automobile. At the same time, an elderly gentleman came out of the shop moving slowly, being impaired with a pronounced limp.

"*Buon giorno! Buon giorno!* The man gushed. Then pointing to the lone table that sat outdoors he invited us to be seated, "*Prego, si accomodi.*" (Good morning. Please, be seated.)

"*Grazie,*" we both replied and sat down.

After we were seated and served, Millie signaled, with a wave of her hand and a nod, for the girls to join her. The girls responded instantly and readily ran to her side. Soon, a mixture of fractured Italian and English words were exchanged in tune with a rash of giggles and waving hands. In the meantime, the elderly gentleman and I traded stories.

A short time later, all five of us became silent when we heard a faint, but growing clip-clop of horse hooves and the rumble of wagon wheels, striking and scraping the cobblestones. The clattering sounds grew louder until they substantially softened the splashed sounds of the nearby fountain, and finally ushering into view a funeral procession.

Six well-groomed black horses, moving with a slow gait, were pulling an ornate white coach that was piled high with floral wreaths. Behind the coach, a long, compact column of men and women followed with the slow pace that was being set by the horses. Except for the young maidens who wore white dresses, all others wore mournful clothing. The women wore the traditional black, ankle-length garment. The men wore a wide, black armband on the left sleeve of their outer clothing. All carried a flower, prayer book or rosary.

After the procession had passed along, Millie turned to the proprietor of the shop and asked, "*Come avviene che il carro, funebre e bianco?*" (How is it that the hearse is white?)

"Musta be like dat. All time white *carro* is for use for small childs anna for girl not yet is married." With a sad facial expression, he nodded his head and softly added, "She be a nice *signorina,* not yet marry. All people in *paese* like her anna come for her *funebre.*"

Certainly, reflected Millie, that accounted for the out-of-character lifeless street and the quiet atmosphere that had greeted them on their early arrival.

Shortly after the procession passed by, we made our goodbyes and resumed the long journey to see the famous monk. It was dark when we reached the city of Bari at the foot of the mountain leading to San Giovanni Rotundo. Negotiating the big automobile during the night and up the narrow winding road was tortuous. With each frightful mile, I became more critical about Padre Pio's purported powers. "If he is so all-knowing and so powerful, why doesn't he make it less difficult for me to take you, his devotee and disciple, up there to see him?"

My continued rant did not draw Millie into a conversation. She remained lax and tolerant. The only time she spoke was when I said a blasphemous word or remark. Then she would say. "That, dear Stan, calls for three Our Fathers and three Hail Marys."

It was ten o'clock at night when we arrived at the village and checked in at the small inn. I was exhausted and high-strung. I plopped on the bed in the cell-like room and huffed, "No thanks to your miracle man, we got here without running off a cliff on that narrow, nanny-goat road." A minute later, still edgy, I got up and said, "I gotta unwind, think I'll go downstairs to read and relax." Leaving the room, I turned and gruffly added, "And don't bother to awaken me for that six o'clock Mass!" Then, with a mumble, I went on, "Guess he starts that early because he doesn't want wide-awake people to really see him." Of course, I was hit with three Our Fathers and three Hail Marys.

The provincial inn was very small and unadorned. It did not offer a conventional foyer as generally expected. The only available public space was a wide passage between the outer door and the three-foot-long reception desk. The only garniture in that space was a small round table with four wooden chairs. The only reading material available was a rumbled four-page newspaper and a frayed booklet reciting the virtues of the town and of Padre Pio. I picked the book up without interest and scanned it idly . . . then it began to grab my complete attention. Shortly after midnight I returned to our room.

Millie awoke at 5:15 A.M. and was surprised to learn that her "Doubting Thomas" intended to accompany her to the morning Mass. She was too elated to seek the reason for the turnabout. Fifteen minutes before the service was to begin, we entered the friary. Taken unawares, every pew in the tiny church was tightly packed with about fifty parishioners. No other seating was available. Stretching up on tiptoe as far as her five-foot, two-inch body would permit, Millie scanned the area from left to right and back again, searching for a spot to squeeze into. The look of disappointment on her face registered that she had found nothing. A young gentleman who was seated nearby detected her anguish and had already sized her up as a *turista*. He arose and graciously surrendered his seat to her, saying, "*Prego, signora, prego.*" I was left just inside the doorway, standing with two other latecomers. Prompted by their good sentiments toward tourists, they welcomed me silently, nodding and smiling as they slid to the side to make room for me.

Unlike the commotion expressed in some of the provincial churches, the only sound that was heard in the packed church was the deep sustained hum mouthed by the peasant women as they recited the rosary. The hum deepened when a man, about forty years of age, wearing a long scapular, appeared, and with a nimble light footing he climbed the three steps to the main altar, lit some candles, and made several other arrangements in preparation for the commencement of the Mass. With the same agility, he descended and disappeared into the sanctum behind the altar.

One of the two men standing in the doorway apparently felt a courteous obligation to pass on to me, a *turista,* the traditional story related to the altar server. He nudged me and whispered, "That man you see on *altare* is made blind when little boy. Some rocks from a big blast when men worked on *strada* make young boy's eyes push out. Padre Pio prays and fixes eyes for boy to see. From little boy he still be long time with Padre Pio in this church." The parishioner, sensing doubt, quickly added, "Siff, you wanna see *prova* . . . is in tribunal to see."

Just then the server appeared again, this time with Padre Pio, who was wearing a white chasuble. The prayerful hum that had filled the church was replaced with gasps of awe as the parishioners knelt, making the sign of the cross. They remained in that kneeling position throughout the Mass, reciting the rosary. Padre Pio's entry and shuffle toward the altar called attention to his feet. It became obvious that the swaddling of multi-layered cloth on each foot caused the dragging and sliding movements. When he came into full view, all eyes riveted on his hands. Like his feet, each hand was heavily bandaged with white cloth.

At this point, the explainer, who was standing next to me, felt the need to impart more background information and describe the wounds of stigmatism. He lowered his head and whispered, "See that he carry much rags on feet and hands. They bleed and bleed. They change the rags and keep old ones in *museo* to see. Even now that he makes seventy years age, you can see blood on rags when he pass here to go out."

Within thirty minutes the Mass was over. Padre Pio left the altar and started up the aisle with a fast shuffle to leave the friary. As he went by, the occupants of each succeeding pew filed into the aisle behind him, murmuring words of blessings. When he reached the exit, he turned his head toward me, nodded and smiled with a stare akin to recognition. The nod, smile and accompanying look caused a trembling motion to ripple through my body. I felt a sensation of being pardoned and blessed . . . I became a believer. (I must add that Padre Pio entered sainthood after his death.)

The following day, we departed San Giovanni

Rotundo and headed southwest through regions of Basilicata and Calabria for 300 miles to Reggio, which sat on the toe of the "Boot." Although I was fluent in Italian and the Neapolitan dialect, I found it difficult to understand or communicate in the local dialect. In spite of that drawback, we met the schedule to board the ferry at Villa Giovanni for Messina. From there, we proceeded south to Taormina and checked in at the Hotel San Domenico, which stood within close range of Mount Etna.

Originally, the San Domenico Hotel was a large quiet monastery. Much of its original structure and decor was maintained when it was converted into a quiet resort. It was so pleasant and comfortable that most visitors made it their base of exploration while touring parts of Sicily.

When awakened on the first morning of our stay, Millie stepped out onto the small bedroom balcony. Her voice, full of excitement, danced back into the bedroom with high-spirited delight.

"Stan, come here! Look at this setting!"

I joined her and was awestruck by the sight. The sweeping view was filled with runaway bougainvillea, manicured orange orchards, lemon groves and vast terraces of multicolored geraniums. A collage of ferns and flowers punctuated every existing nook and niche. The sight caused me to say, "I feel as though I am standing on the side of a huge vase of plants and flowers."

"And, Stan, look how close we are to Mount Etna! I feel that I could reach out and touch it."

"Oh no!" I exclaimed, "You are not going to climb *that* volcano. . . . "

Millie laughed and replied, "I promise not to approach it any closer than this."

That afternoon, we began different trips in a wide circle around the island of Sicily. Millie made certain to include various churches, including the Cefalu Cathedral and the Gibilmanna Sanctuary.

A week later, it was time to depart Sicily and the southern regions of Italy and return to Naples—but not before Millie warmed the heart of a respected padrone and begged an invitation to ride on and drive his donkey-drawn cart. In Sicily, all proud landowners built special wooden carts. They were crafted, painted and polished in a beautiful ornate fashion. Rarely were the colors subdued. Generally, the design of the cart included the family coat of arms. Millie added another regal touch to this landowner's cart as she held the reins and softly goaded the donkey to hasten its pace.

We departed Sicily and headed north. After a long visit at Pompeii, the ancient city that was buried by the outpourings of Mount Vesuvius, we steered for home in Naples. Nearing the southern outskirts of the city, the traffic on the autostrada was slowed to a crawl. The cause was heard before it was seen. Grumbles and bellicose slogans that maligned the Christian Democrat Party strafed the air. The noise became louder as the automobile inched ahead until it was forced to a stop by a mass of protesters.

Judging by their indifferent carriage and vacant facial expressions, a good guess was that a great number of those in the march were passive recruits who held no serious interest in the rally. Obviously they joined and ambled along shoulder to shoulder only with the thought of the advertised free meal and bottle of wine to be had at the end of the day. It was easy to see that the bombastic ranting speech was encouraged by a sprinkle of leading and rabid rabble-rousers who prompted the followers to chant and wave placards and move as slow as the law would permit. Recognizing the ruse for what it was, I knew it would take a long time before the roadway would be cleared. I cut the engine of the automobile, and then, along with the other stymied travelers, just sat and waited.

Throughout the agonizing wait, each separate cluster of captive spectators reacted differently to the encumbrances caused by the antics of the mob. The tight-lipped tourists and the short-time visitors silently scolded the participants for the wrongful interruption of their excursions. Only a few remained completely unmindful of the bothersome impediments.

One local citizen tried to sum it up for the innocent, public-spirited Neapolitans, saying, "Is bad spettacolo, but they musta to do for to show that peoples must have power."

Many minutes crept by before the last vestige of the mob disappeared and headed for another arterial target. It was then that the long line of stalled automobiles, scooters, bicycles, and pedestrians were permitted to pass.

The following day, arriving at our villa, I pulled the car into the courtyard to wash and rid it of the road grime that was sucked onto the wheels and plastered along the body during the trip. The portiere of the villa volunteered to help. His name was Moses, but he always referred to and called himself by the Italian *Mosè*.

A Neapolitan portiere invariably presents himself as an authority in all matters. He acts pleasant while he offers to help with outdoor chores, dispose of the garbage, and clean the driveway. More, he keeps himself well-informed and ready to share whispers about the scuttlebutt he has picked up during the day. Mosè, the portiere of our villa, fit the mold perfectly.

Crouched in a kneeling position, Mosè and I were

scrubbing the chromium-plated wheel spokes, when he asked, "Sor Colonnello, *come e andata I giorni di viaggio?*" (How was the trip?)

"*Bene Bene, Mosè,*" I answered, and then added, "*Fino a ieri.*" (Good, Good, until last evening.)

"*Ma, che successo?*" (But, what happened?)

I went on to recite the nature of the antics shown by the demonstrators. He answered saying "*Che peccato, che peccato, che peccaro* . . . big pity." He shook his head and angrily muttered. "Those people donna like *democrazia.* They make *assemblea* many time to tell people to make like *communista.*"

I knew that Mosè attended the regular assemblages that were called by the leader of the local communistic cell. I always wondered why he, an avowed friend and believer in American ways and customs, attended the gatherings. Now I found an opening to get the answer. With a soft exculpatory tone of voice, I ventured, "But, Mosè, you attend those meetings. Are you a communist?"

"*Ahi, Ahi, Ma No!*" Mosè cried out. "I'ma go with my *compare* jewst for free meal and wine to take to *casa.*"

That expressed the Neapolitan nature and confirmed my belief that most of the marchers in the demonstration were passive participants.

The leave of absence came to an end, and I returned to my duties at Campo Bagnoli. I riffled though the accumulated mail and came across a small envelope addressed to Colonello et Signora D'Amore, Campo Bagnoli. The engraved return address read *Il Santo Ufficio.* I pushed aside all other pieces of correspondence and, with the curiosity and excitement of a child receiving his first valentine, slit the envelope and pulled out a small card that carried four engraved lines:

Your wish to be included among those in a forthcoming personal audience with Pope Pius XII is hereby acknowledged. A Vatican official will contact you about details.

The solemnity reflected by the four lines caused a tingling sensation to ripple through my body. I reread them two more times. I was puzzled. At no time did I look into or request the honor of an audience with the Pope. Unable to logically grasp the reason for the acknowledgment, I called Millie.

"Honey, here's a fast question. Did you ever ask anyone to make arrangements for an audience with the Pope?"

"Heavens, no! That would be pretty cheeky! Why do you ask?"

I proceeded to explain the receipt of the acknowledgment, and she said, "Stan, I have no idea how that came about. I always hoped for such a blessing, and in my prayers to Padre Pio, I did say how grateful I was to see him in person and up so close, and then I said how I longed to see the Pope just as close."

Padre Pio??

Shortly after receiving the announcement, a prelate outlined the system of principles, dress and conduct as they pertained to the forthcoming private audience. Several days later, the same prelate conveyed the word, with a sincere expression of regret, that because of an unforeseen conflict, the private audience was postponed to a later date. Unfortunately we were to depart Italy prior to the newly set date. Hearing this, the prelate made arrangements to include us with an official group that was scheduled for an especial papal reception to be held within the ensuing week.

On the appointed day, I was pleased to see how Millie sparkled with such glorious happiness that was about to explode. We were taken in tow by a guide and escorted through the two huge semicircular porticoes that reached out from Saint Peter's Basilica to embrace the vast piazza—an area capable of holding over 100,000 people. We were led along its length of 1,800 feet into the basilica. Inside, we were escorted through a labyrinth to a narrow ornate rococo corridor, then to a stairway that climbed about fifteen feet to a small loge, which could accommodate no more than ten people. From that position, we in the loge were positioned very close to the pope and had a sweeping view of the interior of the cathedral and the vast crowd of worshippers (about 30,000) who already had crowded inside and front of the papal altar where Pope Pius XII stood to celebrate the Holy Mass.

During the Pope's homily, with welcoming words he called out the name of each person that was seated in the loge. When Millie's name was called, she responded appropriately with two light claps of her hands.

My three-year-tour of duty with NATO came to an end. I was assigned to the Strategic Air Command to take command of a squadron at Bunker Hill, Peru, Indiana. On 24 December 1957, we boarded the luxury liner S.S. *Independence* that departed Naples, Italy for New York, U.S.A.

VI

On my return to the United States, I was transferred to the Strategic Air Command (SAC). On 7 February 1958, I reported for duty at Bunker Hill Air Force Base, Peru, Indiana and given command of a squadron. Bunker Hill was a recent addition to the SAC structure. SAC absorbed it even though it lacked sufficient personnel, proper equipment and type of aircraft to satisfy its assigned mission. A few of the absorbed units with their equipment did meet the basic SAC requirements, however, the demeanor of the personnel was subject to a radical change.

I had been accepted and chosen to command a substandard squadron and bring it up to SAC standards, even though I had less than one year to do the job, because, already, I had been slated for a joint-staff assignment to start on 7 February 1959. Regardless, I was required to get on with the current assignment.

The squadron was comprised of three divisions: Motor, Maintenance, Commercial. The Motor Division carried 330 vehicles of all types, with a group of vehicle operators, to serve all motor vehicle needs on the base. The Maintenance Division held several large garages; a group of mechanics; modern maintenance equipment; and a heavy supply of parts to keep vehicles, including fire trucks, ambulances, refueling tankers and snowplows, in operational readiness. Civil servants manned the Commercial Division. The Division held several warehouses, operated an intra-base diesel railway locomotive, and maintained liaison with the leaders of all civilian modes of transportation—land, air, and sea—to receive and ship cargo and personnel within the United States. Fortunately, competent leaders headed all three divisions; the assigned personnel however, required deeper training in order to meet SAC standards.

Of course, commanding generals of each command demanded perfection to support and accomplish the functions and tasks related to their assigned mission. It was safe to say that the commander of Strategic Air Command demanded more. As a result, a formal authorization was given to all squadron commanders permitting them to give cursory attention to certain bendable regulations and summarily discharge from the service those individuals who demonstrated apathy, lethargy, or poor attitude. I didn't lose time to take advantage of the unique dispensation. Within a few days, I forced a sizable number of misfits "out of the gate." With pride and dedication, the remaining personnel, military and civil, pushed hard to meet the specified goals. Within several months, the squadron won the coveted monthly award, "Outstanding Squadron." And held on to it for months ahead.

A year after taking command of the squadron, I moved on to Dallas, Texas to join a joint Army, Navy, and Air Force staff.

VII

On 7 February 1959, I joined the Southwestern Command of the Military Transportation Management Agency (MTMA). The agency was a relatively new joint Army, Navy, Marine Corps, and Air Force operation; its headquarters was located in Washington, D.C., and commanded by an army major general. It was broken into five regions to cover the forty-eight states. Each region was made responsible to pursue its overall mission in connection with all the military installations located with its geographical area. It was to provide traffic management and service to all of them in connection with the procurement, use, cost and control of high-volume military traffic by commercial means, including: highway, rail, air, pipeline, and waterways within the United States.

The Southwestern Region, with headquarters in Dallas, Texas, was comprised of five states, including Oklahoma, Texas, New Mexico, Arkansas, and Louisiana. It carried a military staff of eight officers—five Army, one Navy and two Air force—plus sixty-seven civil servants, all highly trained technicians in the transportation field. I assumed the position of Deputy Director. My superior, an army colonel, was the Director.

To become more acquainted with the Southwestern Region, I conducted a personal indoctrination survey of all its working components. It was time-consuming and took several weeks to finalize. When completed the thirty-two-page report was not warmly received. It was critical, in that it reflected the feeling that I was not favorably impressed with the mission and the managerial quality with which the assigned functions were preformed. At heart, I felt the function made a detour around governmental law, in that it bargained for a transportation charge or rate lower than that which was previously approved and published by the Interstate Commerce Commission, and which had already been coordinated with the carrier concerned. The nature of such an operation attracted many executives of the transportation industry to call on the local office of the agency with the hope to be rewarded with the targeted traffic provided they offered a lower rate or charge for that particular movement. There were times when if fell upon me to entertain the visitor while the upcoming high-volume traffic was being discussed. I was uncomfortable with that aspect of the duty because of the questionable stratagem and subtlety.

In July 1960, I was promoted to Colonel, Officer Classification: 06. The promotion had no impact pertaining to my assigned tasks. Two years and six months later, my tour of duty with MTNMA was completed. I was assigned to Dover Air Force Base to assume the duty of the Air Traffic Coordinating Officer, ATCO.

VIII

On 31 August 1961, I reported for duty at Dover Air Force Base, Dover, Delaware. To take on the duty as the Air Traffic Coordinating Officer (ATCO).

The Air Force placed an Air Traffic Coordinating Officer at aerial ports where priority cargo was collected for air shipment to further destinations. There were six ATCOs in all to cover the forty eight states. The two main ports were McGuire Air Force Base, New Jersey, and Dover Air Force Base, Dover, Delaware. The other four surrounded the gulf and west coast. I assumed the ATCO duties at Dover Air Force Base.

The main task facing an ATCO was to ensure expeditious movement of the collected material to its intended oversea destination *by its bona-fide predetermined priority.* A highly trained civil staff and a computerized data processing office helped to kept an ongoing watch on every item to make sure it was treated with its intended and given degree priority. However, whatever their processes may have revealed, they were difficult to implement, because of the in-field oppositions. The ATCO was not in the direct chain of command on the Air Base. He was treated somewhat as a tenant on the installation. It was an onerous situation. At times, the position could be considered as being analogous to that of an "outsider" State Policeman who wedges into a proud community to check the proficiency of the duly elected local policemen, and recommend and change what he feels he must do to satisfy *his vested* authority. In spite of the cumbersome aspect of the job, noteworthy advances were made. Against rough odds, additional critical space for processing "Certificate of Acceptance" shipments was secured, and an action to untangle an enormous amount of critical frustrated cargo was made, thereby ensuring that all items would be treated commensurate to their original priority. It wasn't easy, primarily because of constant invasive actions.

One day Millie's wifely awareness prompted her to say, "Stan, for several days you have appeared to fret and brood over something that you are keeping to yourself. What is it?"

Conscience-stricken, I replied in a tone used in a confessional, "I really haven't kept it to myself. On several occasions, I did share my feeling with a couple of our old military friends. I found they feel as I do. We all agreed that the spirit, if not the structure of the military machine, as we knew it years ago, has been seriously weakened by the continuing internal disagreements within and among the offices of higher authority. I feel that we are being directed in a wayward fashion, which I find hard to accept." After a short pause I continued, "I did not want to share these thoughts with you until I felt absolutely certain that I am thinking and planning wisely." Finally, I felt relieved to say, "I miss the old military life. Today it is much different. The zing . . . the feeling of togetherness is gone, especially when you leave the troop level. Hell, for two years with MTMA I felt like a huckster, now I feel like a policeman. For these past three years I performed jobs for business suits not military uniforms. I hate it!" I lowered my head and said just above a whisper, "The way I feel right now is that I should retire before I blow my top." Then I added with a sigh, "Now what do you think of that?"

She was quick to respond. "My dear Stan, we traveled a good part of the world together while you accomplished great things. I followed you for the past twenty-two years. How can I break that bond and that wonderful and exciting way of life now? Just let me know when and where, as you have always done."

The thought and tilt toward retirement was put into motion, silently and slowly. In the meantime, I continued to compile and complete the needed material for an assigned study.

Several months later, after completing the arduous and all-encompassing study that was requested by Headquarters USAF, I received word that a team of two highly rated civil servants would meet with me to pass judgment on the feasibility of immediately implementing the actions suggested in the study. On the appointed day and designated hour, 0800 hours, the ATCO briefing team was seated in the conference room awaiting the arrival of the visiting VIPs.

At 0900 hours, the two officials arrived and entered the room with a cavalier bearing. One had a cigarette dangling from poked-out lips, the other was puffing on a pipe. Both presented themselves in a pompous manner. After a rapid and mechanical introduction, I volunteered a tactful excuse for their late arrival, saying, "I guess you gentlemen had a bad time flying out of Washington this morning."

"No, no, Colonel we flew in last night." The pipe smoker quickly answered. "We went to the Kit Kat Club for dinner and then decided to stay for the floor show." He stopped for a moment, sucked on his pipe, shook his head, chuckled and said "Boy what a joint . . . we had a hell of a time and didn't go to bed until two this morning."

The words hit me like a dagger of disrespect, but I hid it with a feeling of scorn and shrugged it off, saying, "Well, we better get started. We will begin with a background briefing by my staff, and then we will make a field tour. Afterward, we will lunch at the officers' club. After lunch we will go to the docks and observe the newly devised robot cargo-handling operation. Tomorrow morning we will . . . "

The pipe smoker cut in abruptly, "Wait, Colonel, wait. We don't have time for all that! Hell, we are scheduled to fly out of here on tonight's six o'clock flight!" Again, I was taken aback by the words. After a time of silence and with an edge of disgust, I slowly enunciated, with clipped words, "You mean to tell me that you came down here to pass judgment on an innovative study and its related operational aspects, which took weeks to prepare, with your scant five-hour review? Why you spent more time than that at that pussy club!"

The VIP thrust his hands upward in a don't-shoot pose and commanded, "Whoa!" a second later, in a lordly tone, he added, "Colonel, now what in the hell is the big fuss?"

"If I have to explain it to you, it means *nothing*. Instead of continuing on this note, let's cut off the purpose of this visit right now."

Cupping its bowl, the VIP pointed his pipe at me like a pistol, and said, "Careful, Colonel, you're addressing high authority from the Pentagon!"

His manner, tone, and implied warning ticked me off. I replied, "I don't give a damn who you are, or where you're from. And as far as the Pentagon goes, I spent four years there. I know it harbors a lot of pinhead Whiz Kids who have little or no knowledge of the bare-knuckled needs of the military machine." As I spoke, I became more unrestrained and shot out angrily, "And let me tell you this. I will *not* release or discuss my work to anyone who thinks he can appraise a comprehensive study in less time than he spends in a nightclub. You can go back to whomever sent you here and tell him, if he wants to waste your time by sending you on a boondoggle, that's okay with me. But tell him not to waste *my* time by sending you to me." Then, staring into the shock that registered on his face I said, "Got it? Now get the hell out of here. The meeting is over!"

Of course I expected a backlash, but I didn't care. I guess it was because, subconsciously, I welcomed any reason to support my retirement. As expected, several days after the offensive encounter, a general officer called on me. "Colonel, a report that was directed to my office aroused my *interest* concerning your attitude, actions, and unique operation. So I decided to make a stopover here at Dover and get to the bottom of it before heading to the New Orleans port."

Needless to say we had a long, long talk. In the end, he empathized with me. We finished the meeting, and the day, on the golf course . . . where I won all bets.

Happily, I did submit my request for retirement at the end of that year.

THE CONCLUSION

OF AN ACTIVE MILITARY CAREER

" . . . live, laugh, love!"